the now voices

EDITED E

the poetry of the

ANGELO CARLI | THEODORE KILMAN | PALOMAR COLLEGE

present the now voices

CHARLES SCRIBNER'S SONS
New York

ACKNOWLEDGMENTS

On this and pages iv and xii, which constitute an extension of the copy-
right page, acknowledgment is gratefully made to those publishers,
agents, and individuals who have permitted the use of the following
materials in copyright:

For "Fern Hill" and "In My Craft or Sullen Art" by Dylan Thomas,
Collected Poems copyright 1946 by New Directions Publishing Corpora-
tion. Reprinted by permission of New Directions Publishing Corpo-
ration. Canadian rights by permission of J. M. Dent & Sons Ltd and
the trustees for the copyright of the late Dylan Thomas.

For "Sailing" by Susan Murray. Reprinted by permission of the author.

For "The Red Wheelbarrow," Wiliam Carlos Williams, Collected Earlier
Poems. Copyright 1938 by William Carlos Williams. Reprinted by per-
mission of New Directions Publishing Corporation.

For "The Pill Versus the Springhill Mine Disaster" by Richard Brau-

ACKNOWLEDGMENTS

v

tigan. Copyright © 1968 by Richard Brautigan. Reprinted from *The Pill Versus The Springhill Mine Disaster* by Richard Brautigan. A Seymour Lawrence Book/Delacorte Press. Used by permission. First published by Four Seasons Foundation in its Writing series edited by Donald Allen.

For "Senile" and "Empty Holds a Question" by Pat Folk. Reprinted by permission of the author.

For "Dear God, the Day Is Grey" from *Between Wars And Other Poems* by Anne Halley. Reprinted by permission of the University of Massachusetts Press.

For "The Crucifix" and "The Holy Innocents" from *Lord Weary's Castle*, copyright, 1946, by Robert Lowell. Reprinted by permission of Harcourt Brace Jovanovich, Inc. For "Cistercians in Germany" from *Land of Unlikeness* by Robert Lowell. Reprinted by permission of the author. For "The March" by Robert Lowell. Reprinted with the permission of Farrar, Straus & Giroux, Inc. from *Notebook 1967-68* by Robert Lowell, copyright © 1967, 1968, 1969 by Robert Lowell.

For "April Inventory" copyright © 1957 by W. D. Snodgrass. Reprinted from *Heart's Needle*, by W. D. Snodgrass, by permission of Alfred A. Knopf, Inc. For "Winter Bouquet" and "Hometown" by W. D. Snodgrass. Copyright © 1959 by W. D. Snodgrass. Originally appeared in *The New Yorker*. Reprinted by permission of Harper & Row, Publishers. For "The Campus on the Hill" copyright © 1958 by W. D. Snodgrass. Reprinted from *Heart's Needle*, by W. D. Snodgrass, by permission of Alfred A. Knopf, Inc. For "The Lovers Go Fly a Kite" by W. D. Snodgrass in *After Experience*, copyright © 1963 by W. D. Snodgrass. Originally appeared in *The New Yorker*. Reprinted by permission of Harper & Row, Publishers.

For "To W. T. Scott with Thanks for a Poem" and "In Place of a Curse" from *39 Poems* by John Ciardi. Copyright 1959 by Rutgers, The State University. Reprinted by permission of the author. For "On Flunking a Nice Boy out of School" by John Ciardi. Copyright © 1961 Saturday Review, Inc. Reprinted by permission of Saturday Review, Inc. This poem first appeared in the *Saturday Review* April 1, 1961.

For "The Express" by Stephen Spender. Copyright 1934 and renewed 1962 by Stephen Spender. Reprinted from *Selected Poems*, by Stephen Spender, by permission of Random House, Inc. Canadian rights granted by Faber and Faber Ltd.

For "The Voice" (copyright © 1955 by Theodore Roethke), "Light Listened" (copyright © 1964 by Beatrice Roethke), and "My Papa's Waltz" (copyright 1942 by Hearst Magazines, Inc.) from *The Collected Poems of Theodore Roethke*. Reprinted by permission of Doubleday & Company, Inc.

For "Leda and the Swan" by W. B. Yeats. Reprinted by permission of The Macmillan Company from *Collected Poems* by William Butler Yeats. Copyright 1928 by The Macmillan Company, renewed 1956 by Georgie Yeats. Canadian rights granted by E. Michael B. Yeats and The Macmillan Co. of Canada Ltd.

For "chanson innocent" by e.e. cummings. Copyright, 1923, 1951, by e.e. cummings. Reprinted from his volume *Poems 1923-1954*; for "next to of course god" and "a man who had fallen among thieves" by e.e. cummings. Copyright, 1926, by Horace Liveright; copyright, 1954, by e.e. cummings. Reprinted from *Poems 1923-1954* by e.e. cummings; for "if everything happens that can't be done" by e.e. cummings. Copyright, 1944, by e.e. cummings. Reprinted from *Poems 1923-1954* by e.e. cummings; for "anyone lived in a pretty how town" by e.e. cummings. Copyright 1940, by e.e. cummings. Reprinted from his volume *Poems 1923-1954*: by permission of Harcourt Brace Jovanovich, Inc.

For "In California" by Louis Simpson. Copyright © 1961 by Louis Simpson. Reprinted from *At The End of the Open Road*, by Louis Simpson, by permission of Wesleyan University Press. For "Hot Night on Water Street" by Louis Simpson. Copyright © 1957 by Louis Simpson. Reprinted from *A Dream of Governors*, by Louis Simpson, by permission of Wesleyan Press.

For "The Fly" by Karl Shapiro. Copyright 1942 by Karl Shapiro; for "Drug Store" by Karl Shapiro. Copyright 1941 and renewed 1969 by Karl Shapiro; for "University" by Karl Shapiro. Copyright 1940 and renewed 1968 by Karl Shapiro: reprinted from *Selected Poems*, by Karl Shapiro, by permission of Random House, Inc.

For "Out, out—" and "Mending Wall" by Robert Frost. From THE POETRY OF ROBERT FROST edited by Edward Connery Lathem. Copyright 1916, 1930, 1939, © by Holt, Rinehart and Winston, Inc. Copyright 1944, © 1958 by Robert Frost. Copyright © 1967 by Lesley Frost Ballantine; for "The Pasture" from *Complete Poems of Robert Frost* by Robert Frost. Copyright 1939, © 1967 by Holt, Rinehart and Winston, Inc.: reprinted by permission of Holt, Rinehart and Winston, Inc.

For "Santa Claus," "The Dial Tone," "A Picture," "To David about His Education," and "Winter Exercise" from *The Next Room of the Dream* (copyright 1962) by Howard Nemerov; for "The Human Condition" and "Learning by Doing" from *The Blue Swallows* (copyright 1967) by Howard Nemerov; for "Boom!," "Mousemeal," and "Absent-Minded Professor" (copyright 1960, University of Chicago Press) by Howard Nemerov: reprinted by permission of Margot Johnson Agency.

For "Call It a Good Marriage" by Robert Graves. From *Food for Centaurs*, copyright © 1960 by Robert Graves, reprinted by permission

ACKNOWLEDGMENTS

vii   of Collins-Knowlton-Wing, Inc. Published by Doubleday & Company, Inc.

For "The Pioneers" and "Spring Revue" by Charlotte Mortimer. Reprinted by permission of the author.

For "The Love Song of J. Alfred Prufrock" by T. S. Eliot from *Collected Poems 1909-1962*. Reprinted by permission of Harcourt Brace Jovanovich, Inc.

For "The Death of the Ball Turret Gunner" and "A Camp in the Prussian Forest" by Randall Jarrell. Reprinted by permission of Mrs. Randall Jarrell.

For "The Dover Bitch" from *Hard Hours* by Anthony Hecht. Copyright 1960, 1967 by Anthony Hecht. Reprinted by permission of Atheneum Publishers. This poem originally appeared in *The Transatlantic Review*.

For "The Lifeguard" copyright © 1961 by James Dickey. Reprinted from *Drowning with Others*, by James Dickey; for "Them, Crying" copyright © 1964 by James Dickey. Reprinted from *Buckdancer's Choice* by permission of Wesleyan University Press. These poems were first published in *The New Yorker*.

For "Going," "Reasons for Attendance," and "Poetry of Departures" by Philip Larkin are reprinted from *The Less Deceived* copyright © The Marvell Press 1955, 1969 by permission of The Marvell Press, Hessle, Yorkshire, England; for "Essential Beauty" by Philip Larkin. Reprinted by permission of Faber and Faber Ltd. from *The Whitsun Weddings*.

For "Our City Is Guarded by Automatic Rockets" by William Stafford. Copyright © 1958 by William E. Stafford. Reprinted by permission of Harper & Row, Publishers.

For "In a Prominent Bar in Secaucus One Day" from *Nude Descending A Staircase* by X. J. Kennedy. Reprinted by permission of Doubleday & Company, Inc.

For "Constantly risking absurdity" by Lawrence Ferlinghetti, *A Coney Island of the Mind*. Copyright © 1958 by Lawrence Ferlinghetti. Reprinted by permission of New Directions Publishing Corporation.

For "Radar" from *Something of the Sea* by Alan Ross. Reprinted by permission of Houghton Mifflin. Canadian rights granted by Curtis Brown Ltd.

For "Elderly Nobody Erases Self in Central Park" by E. S. Forgotson. Reprinted by permission of *Poetry*: every effort has been made, without success, to locate E. S. Forgotson.

ACKNOWLEDGMENTS

viii   For "A Song for Major Eatherly" from *Weep Before God* by John Wain. Reprinted by permission of St. Martin's Press, Inc. Canadian rights by permission of Macmillan & Co., Ltd., London, and The Macmillan Co. of Canada Ltd.

For "On the Knowledge of Things" by Alexander Taylor. Reprinted by permission from *ETC: A Review of General Semantics Vol. XX, No. 2*; copyright 1963, by the International Society for General Semantics.

For "Person to Person" by Leslie B. Blades. Reprinted by permission from *ETC: A Review of General Semantics* Vol. XVII, No. 2; copyright 1960, by the International Society for General Semantics.

For "Dangling Conversation" by Paul Simon. Copyright © 1966 Paul Simon. Used with permission of Charing Cross Music, Inc.

For "Outside of a Small Circle of Friends" by Phil Ochs. Reprinted by permission of Barricade Music, Inc.

For "Out of Blindness" by Leslie B. Blades. Reprinted by permission from *ETC: A Review of General Semantics, Vol. XVII, No. 2*; copyright 1960, by the International Society for General Semantics.

For "Monologue of a Deaf Man" by David Wright. Reprinted by permission of A. D. Peters & Co. Canadian rights by permission of Andre Deutsch Ltd.

For "Law in the Country of the Cats" from *The Hawk in the Rain* by Ted Hughes. Copyright © 1957 by Ted Hughes.

For "The Dual Site" by Michael Hamburger. Reprinted by permission of Routledge & Kegan Paul Ltd.

For "Love Poem" by Lewis Turco. Reprinted by permission from *ETC: A Review of General Semantics Vol. XVI, No. 3*; copyright· 1959, by the International Society for General Semantics.

For "What's in a Word?" by Carol Shine. Reprinted by permission from *ETC: A Review of General Semantics, Vol. XVII, No. 1*; copyright 1959, by the Inetrnational Society of General Semantics.

For "war war" and "Shot with a Hot Rot Gun" by Michael Goode. Reprinted by permission of the author and the *Village Voice*.

From *In The Mecca* by Gwendolyn Brooks: "Medgar Evers" (copyright © 1964) by Gwendolyn Brooks Blakely; "Malcolm X" and "Boy Breaking Glass" (copyright © 1967) by Gwendolyn Brooks Blakely; "The Blackstone Rangers, Pt. I, As Seen by Disciplines; Pt. II, The Leaders;

CKNOWLEDGMENTS

Pt. III, Gang Girls" (copyright © 1968) by Gwendolyn Brooks Blakely; reprinted by permission of Harper & Row, Publishers, Inc.

For "Foreign Policy Commitments of You Get Into the Catamarian First, Old Buddy" by Paul Blackburn. Reprinted by permission of the author.

For "The Gift of Fire" by Lisel Mueller. Reprinted by permission of the author. First appeared in *Poetry* July 1961.

For "Of Late" from *White Paper* by George Starbuck. Copyright © 1966, by George Starbuck, by permission of Atlantic-Little, Brown and Co. First published in *Poetry* October 1966.

For "Paraders for the Bomb" by Sidney Bernard. Reprinted by permission of the author.

For "Norman Morrison," "Leaflets," and "You Get Used to It" by Adrian Mitchell. Reprinted from *Out Loud* by permission of the author and Cape Cobaid Press. *Out Loud* is distributed in America by Crossman Publishers.

For "Norman Morrison" by David Ferguson. Reprinted by permission of the author.

For "March on the Delta" by Art Berger. Reprinted by permission of the author.

For "1965" by Gibbons Ruark. Reprinted by permission of the author. First appeared in *Poetry* September 1967.

For "Night Riders" by Jean Farley. Reprinted by permission of the author.

For "Winter: For an Untenable Situation," "To a Red-Headed Do-Good Waitress," "On Hurricane Jackson," "What Happened? What Do You Expect," "Morning Song" and "Thesis, Antithesis, and Nostalgia" by Alan Dugan. Reprinted by permission of the author. For "Stability Before Departure" and "Poem" by Alan Dugan. Reprinted by permission of Yale University Press.

For "Going Home" by Tim Reynolds. Reprinted by permission of the author. First appeared in *Poetry* 1967.

For "Orpheus" by Michael Goldman. Reprinted by permission of the author and the *Kenyon Review*.

For "Birmingham Sunday" by Richard Farina (© Ryerson Music Publishers, Inc. 1964). Reprinted by permission of Ryerson Music Publishers, Inc.

ACKNOWLEDGMENTS

x

For "Testimonies for a School Prayer" by Serge Gavronsky. Reprinted by permission of the author.

For "Women in Brooklyn" by Paul Zweig. Reprinted by permission of the author. First appeared in *Poetry* September 1967.

For "Contemporary Fear" by Don Ober. Reprinted by permission of the author.

For "19??" by Dan Georgakas. Reprinted by permission of the author.

For "On Seeing a Stamp from the Democratic Republic of Vietnam" by Leslie Woolf Hedley. Reprinted by permission of the author.

For "The Art of Poetry" by Dennis Trudell. Reprinted by permission of the author. Appeared in *Quickly Aging Here* (Doubleday/Anchor 1969).

For "In Mexico" by Robert Sward. Reprinted by permission of the author.

For "I Looked over Jordan" by Lane Dunlop. Reprinted by permission of the *Yale Review*, copyright Yale University. First appeared in the *Yale Review*.

For "Poem No. 27," "Poem No. 929," "Poem No. 078," "Poem No. 105," and "Poem No. 140" by RCA 301. Reprinted by permission of RCA *Electronic Age*.

For "A Week in Paradise" by John Ridland. Reprinted by permission of the author.

For "The Family Goldschmitt" by Henri Coulette. Reprinted by permission of the author.

For "The Corridor" and "On the Move" by Thom Gunn. Reprinted by permission of Faber and Faber Ltd. from *The Sense of Movement.* For "Black Jackets" from *My Sad Captains* by Thom Gunn by permission of The University of Chicago Press. Canadian rights by permission of Faber and Faber Ltd.

For "Highway 101, Seal Beach" by Curtis Zahn. Reprinted by permission from *ETC: A Review of General Semantics Vol. XIX, No. 4*; copyright 1963, by the International Society for General Semantics.

For "Incident" from *On These I Stand* by Countee Cullen. Copyright 1925 by Harper & Row Brothers, renewed 1953 by Ida M. Cullen. Reprinted by permission of Harper & Row, Publishers.

For "In Praise of BIC Pens" and "The Poet Tries to Turn in His Jock' from *The Shot Goes In* (Quixote Press, Madison, 1969). Reprinted by permission of the author. Appeared in *Quickly Aging Here* (Doubleday/Anchor, 1969).

For "Good Luck to You Kafka/You'll Need It Boss" from the book of the same title (Rapp & Whiting: May 1969) by Henry Graham. Reprinted by permission of the author and *Evergreen Review*.

For "In America" and "The Student" by Marianne Moore. Reprinted by permission of The Macmillan Company from *Collected Poems* by Marianne Moore. Copyright 1941 by Marianne Moore, renewed 1969 by Marianne Moore and T. S. Eliot.

For "The Student" by Dabney Stuart. Copyright © 1966 by Dabney Stuart. Reprinted from *In a Particular Place*, by Dabney Stuart, by permision of Alfred A. Knopf, Inc.

For "The Three Movements" by Donald Hall. From *The Dark House*, copyright © 1957 by Donald Hall. Published by The Viking Press, Inc. Reprinted by permission of Curtis-Brown, Ltd.

For "Classes" from *Graves Registry and Other Poems* by Keith Wilson. Published by Grove Press, Inc. Copyright © 1966, 1967, 1968, and 1969 by Keith Wilson.

For "Education" by Kenneth Rexroth. Reprinted by permission of the author and New Directions Publishing Corporation. First published in *Poetry* December 1966.

For "University Examinations in Egypt" from *Laughing Hyena* by D. J. Enright. Reprinted by permission of Routledge & Kegan Paul Ltd.

For "Kindergarten Teacher" by Stanley Kiesel. Reprinted by permission of the author.

For "On Returning to Teach" by Marvin Bell. Reprinted by permission of the author.

For "Grief" and "Constructions: Upper East Side" from *Manhattan Pastures* by Sandra Hochman. Copyright © 1963 by Yale University. Reprinted by permission of Yale University Press.

For "Cold Water Flat" from *Letter from a Distant Land* by Philip Booth. Copyright 1953 by Philip Booth. Reprinted by permission of The Viking Press, Inc.

For "The Bay Ridge from Portrero Hill" and "Malvolio in San Francisco" by Jack Gilbert. Copyright © 1962 by Yale University. Reprinted by permission of Yale University Press.

For "Ditty" by Roger Hecht from *27 Poems*, the Swallow Press Incorpo-

ACKNOWLEDGMENTS

xii   rated, 1964, originally appearing in the *Kenyon Review*, Autumn, 1964. Reprinted by permission of the Swallow Press Incorporated.

For "Working on Wall Street" (copyright © 1956 May Swenson) by May Swenson. Reprinted by permission of Charles Scribner's Sons from *To Mix with Time*.

For "An Urban Convalescence" from *Water Street* by James Merrill. Copyright © 1960 by James Merrill. Reprinted by permission of Atheneum Publishers. Originally appeared in *Partisan Review*.

For "Depression" by William Witherup. Reprinted by permission of the author. Appeared in *Prairie Schooner*.

For "The Journey of a Poem Compared to All the Sad Variety of Travel" by Delmore Schwartz. Reprinted by permission of Kenneth A. Schwartz. First appeared in *Kenyon Review*.

For "Carmen Saeculare" by John Taylor. Reprinted by permission of the author.

For "The Honored Dead" by Thomas Doulis. Reprinted by permission of Gunther Stuhlmann.

reface

The poet dedicates himself to the task of touching people and moving them—intellectually, emotionally, aesthetically. It is therefore paradoxical that English instructors find it so difficult to interest students in the study of poetry. Far from being moved and touched, students generally have only a marginal interest in poetry. Instructors look upon the teaching of poetry as a task—often insurmountable —a task of stimulating, motivating, involving, of subtly coercing students to read, to be touched, to be moved by poetry.

What is it about the contemporary student, present-day teaching methods, poetry itself, that produces student antipathy toward poetry? Before this question can be answered, one must understand something of the nature of today's college student. The new student is action-oriented, interested in the *NOW*, and concerned with contemporary problems and social issues. He sees the present-day world demanding responses from him; he sees the future of the world as dependent upon his moral assertions; he sees people caught in the morass of social injustice calling for his help; he finds the world around him compelling. In his rush to deal head-on with the world's contemporary problems, he views the study of poetry and its traditions with a jaundiced eye.

Poetry to many of these new students is a language of the past only. Semester after semester students are exposed, re-exposed, and eventually over-exposed to the same well known, critically "safe" poets—Milton, Shakespeare, Dryden, Pope, Wordsworth, Coleridge, Keats, Shelly, Arnold, Yeats, Eliot. In spite of the greatness of these poets, they often fail to speak to the student of today in his own language, in terms of his own experience. Not only are the words of the poems archaic to the student's ear, but he has difficulty identifying with issues and circumstances that he considers irrelevant for today's fast-changing society. He remains untouched by issues presented in the dress of bygone eras.

Yet for the student to appreciate poetry, he *must* be touched by the poet—something must be said to *him*. Before a poem can move him, there must be some common ground between the poem and the student. The place to begin the study of poetry is with poems written in the language of the reader: the student should begin with poems of his own time and his own language. Consequently, the poems in this collection reflect the action, mores, values, and social temper of this age. They are the poems of contemporary individuals living, being influenced by, and reacting to this period in history. The concerns, fears, and hopes of these poets are the concerns, fears, and hopes of the new student; concerns which are reflected in this anthology by such topics as communications, dissent, identity, education, and the city.

The poems deal with topics which deeply affect modern man, and they do so in a language and form the students can understand. Note, for example, that the contemporary folk ballad is presented; this is part of the student's experience; it is something with which he can identify. By developing an understanding of the ballads recorded by Phil Ochs, Simon and Garfunkel, and others, the student gains insights into the ballad form and finally finds a point of reference for the appreciation and understanding of the traditional ballad as well, if the instructor chooses to present it. Thus, modern poetic structures and contemporary poetic language may serve as the gateway to the acceptance of all poetry by today's student.

One realizes that there is a certain amount of risk involved in compiling such an anthology. Obviously, one cannot determine if this is the best of all contemporary poetry, much less anticipate which, if any, will achieve immortality. Those questions may only be answered, if at all, by posterity. Only by looking back can anyone clearly determine what was the best poetry of any time, and looking back is certainly not the concern of this work. All that can be said is that the poems selected are poems which, in the judgment of the authors, are good poems, worthy of the student's time and study. They are poems of the moment, providing common ground for discussion between instructor and student, in terms of both the subject matter and the genre.

Contents

EDUCATION

the now voices

THE LANGUAGE OF POETRY

INTRODUCTION

Many students come to poetry with a lack of interest in the subject because of various preconceptions they have of it. They are convinced that, among other things, poetry is effeminate, mysterious, full of "hidden" meanings, and consequently impossible to understand. The fact of the matter is that poetry is frequently beautiful, intellectually stimulating, emotionally moving, informative, and just plain fun.

The popular misconceptions about poetry arise, in part at least, from the fact that poetry is written in a different form from that with which people are most familiar—prose. The form, with its dependency upon figurative language and rhythmic regularity—resulting in a visually unfamiliar structure—tends to inhibit the beginning reader, discouraging him

4   from pursuing the study of poetry to any significant end. But is it not foolish to be intimidated by an unfamiliar form of expression and therefore deprived of some very pleasurable aesthetic moments? The wise individual learns all about the form so that he may use it to achieve the experience the poem is offering him. After all, it is primarily through the form that the poet makes *concrete* the idea, the emotion, the experience (all abstractions) that he is trying to communicate. In fact, the reader has a *responsibility*, both to himself and to the poet, to familiarize himself with the characteristics of the genre before passing judgment on its communicative value. When he has satisfied that responsibility, he is likely to discover that poetry is a very sensitive, very precise, and often a very complete expression of the world in which he lives. If he continues to examine poetry in all its various aspects, he will eventually achieve that ideal state in which he will become so familiar with the techniques or devices of poetry that he no longer consciously considers them when he is responding to the poem; they will have become a part of his nature, wherein they operate almost intuitively whenever he is considering a poem. At this point, his response to and understanding of poetry will be as effortless as the poem itself appears to be. One might say that learning to read poetry is like learning to understand and thereby more fully appreciate a piano concerto. One who knows nothing about music is necessarily limited in his understanding and appreciation of the performance of a work. But one who has practiced the piano until technique has become ingrained in him will apply his experience in achieving a greater understanding and appreciation of the performance he is witnessing. Though most of us may never achieve this ideal state, either as pianists or poets, any attempt to do so will bring us closer to the complete artistic experience than if we did nothing at all.

In the discussion which is to follow, great care has been taken to select examples that illustrate the figurative language of this time and place. Modern poetry is full of things that have never appeared in verse before, either because they never existed before and are entirely products of contemporary society or, if existing before, were never thought to be emotionally suggestive enough to have any great poetic value. Patients etherized upon a table, analysts, knots of hair that clog the drains, the drugstore, the drive-in church, the children's television program, all have a dramatic force in direct proportion to their significance in today's world. At the same time, one cannot ignore the illustrative value of certain traditional poems and poets; consequently, some conventional examples have been included in order to best describe various poetic devices, and to further dramatize the unique qualities of contemporary verse.

Groups of poems have been periodically included throughout so that the student may study and apply what he has learned from the preceding discussion; this provides the student with an opportunity to test his understanding of the theories previously presented. Each group of poems has been organized primarily to illustrate those details covered in the period since the previous bloc of verse; obviously, however, all the poems contain, and therefore may be used to discuss, poetic techniques presented elsewhere in the chapter.

The most important element of poetry with which one should become familiar is its language, for language is the "stuff" of poetry. It is in the nature of poetry to compress the expression of ideas, emotions, and sensations, so that a great impact is made and understanding achieved in the fewest possible words; this economy is achieved primarily by creating an image, either descriptive or figurative, of the poet's intent. Joseph Conrad once said that the task of the writer is "by the power of the written word, to make you hear, to make you feel . . . to make you see." This is how *imagery* works in verse. Literally, *imagery* refers to descriptive passages, passages which appeal entirely to the senses in their vividness and detail. The pleasure derived from such passages is much like that derived from the splash of color in a New England fall or the singing of a meadowlark in summer. Dylan Thomas' "Fern Hill" and Susan Murray's "Sailing" are poems that provide just this kind of pleasure through vivid, sensual detail.

Poetry

Fern Hill

Now as I was young and easy under the apple boughs
About the lilting house and happy as the grass was green,
    The night above the dingle starry,
        Time let me hail and climb
    Golden in the heydays of his eyes,
And honoured among wagons I was prince of the apple towns
And once below a time I lordly had the trees and leaves
        Trail with daisies and barley
    Down the rivers of the windfall light.

And as I was green and carefree, famous among the barns
About the happy yard and singing as the farm was home,
    In the sun that is young once only,
        Time let me play and be
    Golden in the mercy of his means,
And green and golden I was huntsman and herdsman, the
        calves
Sang to my horn, the foxes on the hills barked clear and cold,
        And the sabbath rang slowly
    In the pebbles of the holy streams.

All the sun long it was running, it was lovely, the hay
Fields high as the house, the tunes from the chimneys, it was air
    And playing, lovely and watery
        And fire green as grass.
    And nightly under the simple stars
As I rode to sleep the owls were bearing the farm away,
All the moon long I heard, blessed among stables, the nightjars
    Flying with the ricks, and the horses
        Flashing into the dark.

And then to awake, and the farm, like a wanderer white
With the dew, come back, the cock on his shoulder: it was all
    Shining, it was Adam and maiden,
        The sky gathered again
    And the sun grew round that very day.
So it must have been after the birth of the simple light
In the first, spinning place, the spellbound horses walking warm
    Out of the whinnying green stable
        On to the fields of praise.

And honoured among foxes and pheasants by the gay house
Under the new made clouds and happy as the heart was long,
    In the sun born over and over,
        I ran my heedless ways,
    My wishes raced through the house high hay
And nothing I cared, at my sky blue trades, that time allows
In all his tuneful turning so few and such morning songs
    Before the children green and golden
        Follow him out of grace.

Nothing I cared, in the lamb white days, that time would take
    me
Up to the swallow thronged loft by the shadow of my hand,
    In the moon that is always rising,
        Nor that riding to sleep
    I should hear him fly with the high fields

8   And wake up to the farm forever fled from the childless land.
Oh as I was young and easy in the mercy of his means,
   Time held me green and dying
  Though I sang in my chains like the sea.

DYLAN THOMAS

Sailing

Come Spring, when clouds
are whipped to white-capped froth,
spiders spin their fragile
rigging webs against the scudding wind
which flings those first,
fine thread lines up,
up beyond the bud furled
tips of Chinese Elms as
though the bouyant breeze,
fitted out with only
silken lines,
could moor the very sky—
to trees.

SUSAN MURRAY

But one can easily see that the value of imagery in poetry does not end at this sensual level, for words which convey sensory impressions often achieve a vividness, and thereby an emotional impact, unattainable through more abstract expression, and herein lies the ultimate value for the poets of imagery-bearing language. For the end of such vivid language, as Conrad goes on to say, is to present an experience, "To show its vibration, its color, its form and through its movement, its form, its color, reveal the substance of its truth—disclose the inspiring secret: the stress and passion within the core of each convincing moment;" in other words, crystallize for us things which are of the mind and of the heart. This kind of imagery is not static but blossoms to suggest the multi-dimensional levels of meaning inherent in great poetry. When, in "The Love Song of J. Alfred Prufrock," Prufrock suddenly says:

> I should have been a pair of ragged claws
> Scuttling across the floors of silent seas

the poet has evoked an image which says, in effect, "I am incapable of being a man, walking tall, upright, in the sunlight, in the world of men. Rather, I am qualified to be a lesser form of life, a scavenger after waste, crawling in a world of darkness and silence." This in turn can be reasonably extended to mean, "I lack conviction. I lack the kind of courage which defines man. I am, in fact, cowardly." The kind of compressive language illustrated by Eliot's image is referred to generally as *figurative language,* language which is extremely connotative and which carries the reader to levels of meaning other than the literal. More specifically, this figurative language is classified under such terms as simile, metaphor, symbol, personification, allusion, hyperbole, metonymy, synechdoche, tone.

The earlier analogy of the pianist is a form of simile. It is an attempt to describe or explain an unknown quantity in terms of a better known, albeit somewhat different quantity. When a simile is employed, the poetic comparison is stated, and such statement is characterized by the use of "as," "like," "resembling," and similar terms. The opening lines of "Prufrock" contain a classic example of this kind of comparison:

> Let us go then, you and I
> When the evening is spread out against the sky
> Like a patient etherized upon a table;

The metaphor is also a comparative term, but in this case, the comparison is implied. The metaphor, probably more

10 than any other rhetorical device, represents what Robert Frost has defined the nature of poetry to be: ". . . the one permissible way of saying one thing and meaning another." This figure of speech is a word or a group of words that ordinarily mean one thing but that, when presented in the context of a poem, mean something else, something not necessarily related to the literal or usual meaning. In any case, the relation between the literal and the implied meaning is usually understood, not expressed. Perhaps the clearest explanation of metaphor is that of I. A. Richard's *Philosophy of Rhetoric* wherein he introduced the terms *tenor* and *vehicle*. The *vehicle* is the word of words themselves, the *tenor* is what the words connote to the reader. In the case of the crab image discussed earlier, for example, the ragged claws scuttling across the floors of silent seas is the vehicle whereby the tenor, all that was stated in paraphrase, is communicated. Or when Shakespeare says in Sonnet 73

> That time of year thou may'st in me behold
> When yellow leaves, or none, or few, do hang
> Upon those boughs which shake against the cold,
> Bare ruined choirs, where late the sweet birds sang.

he is metaphorically speaking, with "Bare ruined choirs, where late the sweet birds sang" (vehicle), of barren, windblown, winter trees (tenor).

A more extended and more complex example of this poetic device may be found in Alfred Hayes' "The Slaughter-House." In this poem, the entire second stanza, a vividly detailed extension of the title, might be said to be a metaphor, a vehicle for presenting a poetic view of how man is treated in the contemporary world (tenor).

11   The Slaughter-House

Under the big 500-watted lamps, in the huge sawdusted
    government inspected slaughter-house,
head down from hooks and clamps, run on trolleys over
    troughs,
the animals die.
Whatever terror their dull intelligences feel
    or what agony distorts their most protruding eyes
the incommunicable narrow skulls conceal.

Across the sawdusted floor,
ignorant as children, they see the butcher's slow
    methodical approach
in the bloodied apron, leather cap above, thick square
    shoes below,
struggling to comprehend this unique vision upside down,
and then approximate a human scream
    as from the throat slit like a letter
the blood empties, and the windpipe, like a blown valve,
    spurts steam.

But I, sickened equally with the ox and lamb,
    misread my fate,
mistake the butcher's love
    who kills me for the meat I am
to feed a hungry multitude beyond the sliding doors.
    I, too, misjudge the real
purpose of this huge shed I'm herded in: not for my love
    or lovely wool am I here,
but to make some world a meal.
    See, how on the unsubstantial air
I kick, bleating my private woe,

as upside down my rolling sight
somersaults, and frantically I try to set my world upright;
        too late learning why I'm hung here,
whose nostrils bleed, whose life runs out from eye and ear.

ALFRED HAYES

Interestingly enough, both Shakespeare and Hayes employ symbols in the development of their themes. A symbol may be defined as a concrete object of action (anything perceived through the senses) used to represent an abstract concept. In the Shakespeare excerpt, that time of year that is referred to, late fall or winter, traditionally symbolizes the approaching end to life for things in nature. Therefore, in this poem, the shedding of the leaves, the shaking against the cold (concrete occurrences) represent the passages of time (abstraction) for the poet. Similarly, in Hayes' poem, the sheep (concrete) symbolizes man in his innocence (abstraction), while the slaughter-house (concrete) represents the world in its bestiality (abstraction).

Hayes also makes use of another poetic device—personification—which attributes human characteristics to inanimate objects, animals, idea. Personification functions as a metaphor in which the figurative, personifying term is substituted for the literal term. In "The Slaughter-House," for example, the personal and very human pronoun "I" is substituted for sheep. This pronoun brings with it all the qualities usually associated primarily with man—in this case, the capacity to reason, to understand, to respond emotionally to the situation at hand.

In light of all that has been determined from the imagery of Hayes' stanza (and this is not to imply that the subject has been exhausted), it would not be unreasonable to suggest that the second stanza of his poem metaphorically and symbolically broadens to include still another level of meaning—the ordeal of Christ on the Cross. The symbol of the lamb,

13 the "hungry multitude beyond the sliding doors," mistaking the butcher's love, misjudging the real purpose of this huge shed (world) he is herded into, hanging upside down (the traditional Roman manner of crucifixion), bleeding from eye and ear, yet still frantically trying to set his world upright, all echo Christ's purpose and reward on this earth. Thus, one may reasonably progress from understanding the poem as descriptive of how individual man is sacrificed, of innocent man's ordeal in the world, to an understanding of the poem as descriptive of *the* most innocent man's sacrifice and agony in this world—all the result of imagery which is not static, and which blossoms to suggest multi-dimensional levels of meaning.

Now examine the multi-dimensional aspects of the poems immediately following by distinguishing between and closely examining the devices of presentation employed by the poets: simile, metaphor, symbol, and personification among others.

Clarify the differences between metaphor and symbol. Is "The Red Wheelbarrow" metaphoric or symbolic? How does the kite in the Snodgrass poem and "green" in the Ciardi poem function? How does the personification of "The Express" add to its metaphoric value?

Poetry

The Red Wheelbarrow

So much depends
upon

a red wheel
barrow

glazed with rain
water

beside the white
chickens

WILLIAM CARLOS WILLIAMS

The Pill Versus the Springhill Mine Disaster

When you take your pill
it's like a mine disaster.
I think of all the people
    lost inside of you.

RICHARD BRAUTIGAN

Senile

His tundra'd mind sprouts leaflets
here and there
and causes me to stare
in new awareness of the man
he must have been.
Where he now
         struggles
                  to retain
such meagre lichen to his brain
he must have raised
rare orchids
years ago.

PAT FOLK

Dear God, the Day is Grey

Dear God, the day is grey. My house
is not in order. Lord, the dust
sifts through my rooms and with my fear,
I sweep mortality, outwear
my brooms, but not this leaning floor
which lasts and groans. I, walking here,
still loathe the labors I would love
and hate the self I cannot move.

And God, I know the unshined boards,
the flaking ceiling, various stains
that mottle these distempered goods,
the greasy cloths, the jagged tins,
the dog that paws the garbage cans.
I know what laborings, love, and pains,

16　　my blood would will, yet will not give:
the knot of hair that clogs the drains
clots in my throat. My dyings thrive.

The refuse, Lord, that I put out
burns in vast pits incessantly.
All piecemeal deaths, trash, undevout
and sullen sacrifice, to thee.

ANNE HALLEY

The Crucifix

How dry time screaks in its fat axle-grease,
As spare November strikes us through the ice
And the Leviathan breaks water in the rice
Fields, at the poles, at the hot gates to Greece;
It's time: the old unmastered lion roars
And ramps like a mad dog outside the doors,
Snapping at gobbets in my thumbless hand.
The seaways lurch through Sodom's knees of sand
Tomorrow. We are sinking. "Run, rat, run,"
The prophets thunder, and I run upon
My father, Adam. Adam, if our land
Become the desolation of a hand
That shakes the Temple back to clay, how can
War ever change my old into new man?
Get out from under my feet, old man. Let me pass;
On Ninth Street, through the Hallowe'en's soaped glass,
I picked at an old bone on two crossed sticks
And found, to *Via et Vita et Veritas*
A stray dog's signpost is a crucifix.

ROBERT LOWELL

Winter Bouquet

Her hands established, last time she left my room,
this dark arrangement for a winter bouquet:
collected bittersweet, brittle stemmed Scotch broom,
perennial straw-flowers, grasses gone to seed,
lastly, the dry vaginal pods of milkweed.
These relics stay here for her when she's away.

Bulging like a coin purse fallen on the ground
of damp woods, overgrained with moss, mould and frost,
their husks are horned like the Venus-combs I found
on Garipan. Those war years, many a wife
wandered the fields after such pods to fill life
preservers so another man might not be lost.

Now she's home. Today I lifted them, like charms
in the March sunshine to part the pods and blow
white bursts of quilly weedseed for the wide arms
and eyes of the children squealing where they drift
across the neighbors' cropped lawns like an airlift
of satyrs or a conservative, warm snow.

W. D. SNODGRASS

The Lovers Go Fly a Kite

What's up, today, with our lovers?
    Only bright tatters—a kite
That plunges and bobs where it hovers
    At no improbable height.

18   It's shuddery like a hooked fish
    Or stallion. They reel in string
And sprint, compassing their wish:
    To keep in touch with the thing.

They tear up their shirts for a tail
    In hopes that might steady
It down. Wobbling, frail,
    They think it may not be ready

And balance their hawk aloft—
    Poor moth of twigs and tissue
That would spill if one child wind coughed,
    Dive down to tear, or to kiss you,

Yet still tugs the line they keep
    Like some exquisite sting ray
Hauled from a poisonous deep
    To explore the bright coasts of day.

Or say it's their weather ear
    Keeping the heart's patrol of
A treacherous, washed-out year,
    Searching for one sprig of olive.

What air they breathe is wrung
    With twenty subtleties;
Sharp bones of failure, hung
    In all the parkway trees;

It's enough to make you laugh—
    In these uncommitted regions
On an invisible staff
    To run up an allegiance!

                                      W. D. SNODGRASS

To W. T. Scott

with thanks for a poem

I like that poem, Win. There's a green world in it.
Not just green acreage—any nature boy
can rhyme on that a dozen lines a minute:
put in a bluebird if you're out for joy,
put in a hayloft if you're out for plot,
put in a dead tree if you're out for thought.

I mean what's green in being what a man
touches to leave. Say, Mark Twain at the end;
the green of his last thought. Suppose it ran
to Huck or Jim drifting around a bend;
then stopped there with a sigh or with a smile,
or even wondering had it been worthwhile,

but still a life to think about that stood
green to itself. As God might lose a world
yet think back and be sad that it was good.
All green dies. But the sere manfingers curled
to their last pulse, touch in a memory.
Touch, and I think are justified. For me

that green is first. The green thought more than green
of Walden is Thoreau. The man unspared.
As queer as he was green. An in-between:
half-Cod, half-Buddha. But a system bared
to its own pulse. He had a mind with wings.
But best of all he had an eye for things.

God, how he could see green! He must have died
with time ablaze around him like spring fern

20   caught in a single ray of sun inside
a glacier-rumpled Stonehenge, while a churn
of swallows buttered him his last of light.
—All nothing till he held it in his sight.

That green. Say, Whitman like a stricken bear
thinking: "What is a sea?" Say, Henry James
thinking: "What country is it over there?"
on a long foggy walk beside the Thames.
Say, Melville thinking: "What have I left done
that will stay green to time for anyone?"

And *all* done. What a sea or country is.
What world can grow to, shaped round from the mind.
Such forests deeper than Yosemites
a man walks thinking in and leaves behind.
That last green, Win, after the first unrolled.
The eighth day of the world, by a man told.

JOHN CIARDI

The Express

After the first powerful plain manifesto
The black statement of pistons, without more fuss
But gliding like a queen, she leaves the station.
Without bowing and with restrained unconcern
She passes the houses which humbly crowd outside,
The gasworks and at last the heavy page
Of death, printed by gravestones in the cemetery.
Beyond the town there lies the open country
Where, gathering speed, she acquires mystery,
The luminous self-possession of ships on ocean.
It is now she begins to sing—at first quite low
Then loud, and at last with a jazzy madness—

1
The song of her whistle screaming at curves,
Of deafening tunnels, brakes, innumerable bolts.
And always light, aerial, underneath
Goes the elate metre of her wheels.
Steaming through metal landscape on her lines
She plunges new eras of wild happiness
Where speed throws up strange shapes, broad curves
And parallels clean like the steel of guns.
At last, further than Edinburgh or Rome,
Beyond the crest of the world, she reaches night
Where only a low streamline brightness
Of phosphorus on the tossing hills is white.
Ah, like a comet through flame she moves entranced
Wrapt in her music no bird song, no, nor bough
Breaking with honey buds, shall ever equal.

STEPHEN SPENDER

Light Listened

O what could be more nice
Than her ways with a man?
She kissed me more than twice
Once we were left alone.
Who'd look when he could feel?
She'd more sides than a seal.

The close air faintly stirred.
Light deepened to a bell,
The love-beat of a bird.
She kept her body still
And watched the weather flow.
We live by what we do.

All's known, all, all around:
The shape of things to be;

22   A green thing loves the green
And loves the living ground.
The deep shade gathers night;
She changed with changing light.

We met to leave again
The time we broke from time;
A cold air brought its rain,
The singing of a stem.
She sang a final song;
Light listened when she sang.

THEODORE ROETHKE

    Two additional types of poetic "vehicles" (see Metaphor, p. 9) are synecdoche and metonymy. Synecdoche occurs when the poet uses an integral part of something to represent the total object, or vice versa. When Robert Lowell says in "Mr. Edwards and the Spider," "How will the hands grow strong? How will the heart endure?" or in "The Dead in Europe," "Not grilled and spindle spires pointing to heaven could save us," he is referring to the whole man and to the church structure respectively.

    The distinction between synecdoche and metonymy is so slight as to confuse most readers, with the result that metonymy is more and more frequently used to describe both types of metaphor. However, the distinction does exist and should be described. Metonymy occurs when something *closely associated* with an idea or experience, but not necessarily an integral part of that idea, is used to represent the entire idea. The keys to this distinction lie in the words "integral part = total object" (synecdoche) and "closely associated with = total idea" (metonymy). An example of metonymy is:

"He wore his crown wisely" = He ruled wisely"
crown = rule

23   People are sometimes further confused by the seeming similarity between metonymy and symbol. The distinction here is that in metonymy the *figure of speech* has some relationship to the total idea or experience it represents, while the symbol need not. In "He wore his crown wisely," the crown is closely associated with "ruling" in a very real sense (metonymy). On the other hand, there is no *real* relationship between the "dove" and that which is traditionally symbolizes, "peace" (symbol).

The specific nature of metonymy and synecdoche makes them both effective poetic tools. An understanding of their poetic function will help the student to respond *precisely* as the poet intends he should wherever these figures are used in a work.

The following three poems make notable use of metonomy and synecdoche. The nature of each of these poetic devices and the distinction between them will be readily seen when analyses of the poems themselves are undertaken.

Poetry

The Voice

One feather is a bird,
I claim; one tree, a wood;
In her low voice I heard
More than a mortal should;
And so I stood apart,
Hidden in my own heart.

And yet I roamed out where
Those notes went, like the bird,
Whose thin song hung in air,
Diminished, yet still heard:
I lived with open sound,
Aloft, and on the ground.

That ghost was my own choice,
The shy cerulean bird;
It sang with her true voice,
And it was I who heard
A slight voice reply;
I heard; and only I.

25   Desire exults the ear:
Bird, girl, and ghostly tree,
The earth, the solid air—
Their slow song sang in me;
The long noon pulsed away,
Like any summer day.

THEODORE ROETHKE

Cistercians in Germany

Here corpse and soul go bare. The Leader's headpiece
Capers to his imagination's tumblings;
The Party barks at its unsteady fledglings
To goose-step in red-tape, and microphones
Sow the four winds with babble. Here the Dragon's
Sucklings tumble on steel-scales and puff
Billows of cannon-fodder from the beaks
Of bee-hive camps, munition-pools and scrap-heaps,
And here the serpent licks up Jesus' blood,
Valhalla vapors from the punctured tank.
Rank upon rank the cast-out Christians file
Unter den Linden to the Wilhelmsplatz,
Where Caesar paws the gladiator's breast;
His martial bumblings and hypnotic yawp
Drum out the pastors of these aimless pastures;
And what a muster of scarred hirelings and scared sheep
To cheapen and popularize the price of blood!

But who will pipe of pastors, herds and hirelings
Where a strait-laced mechanic calls the tune?
Here the stamped tabloid, ballot, draft or actress
Consumes all access and all faculties
For spreading blandishments or terror. Here
Puppets have heard the civil words of Darwin

26   Clang clang, while the divines of screen and air
Twitter like Virgil's harpies eating plates,
And lions scamper up the rumps of sheep.
The Shepherd knows his sheep have gone to market;
Sheep need no pastoral piping for the kill,
Only cold mutton and a fleecing.

The milch-goat gave two tuns of mead a day:
Germans, you swallow this. Flint-headed hearts,
You have forgotten Adam's fault and howl:
"Who was this man who sowed the dragon's teeth,
This fabulous or fancied patriarch
Who sowed so ill for his descent? This ulcer
Our ghettoes isolate but cannot purge?
God's blood be on the bankers and the Jews."
Yesterday pagan Junkers smashed our cells,
We lift our bloody hands to wizened Bernard,
To Bernard gathering his canticle of flowers,
His soul a bridal chamber fresh with flowers,
And all his body one ecstatic womb,
And through the trellis peers the sudden Bridegroom.

ROBERT LOWELL

My Papa's Waltz

The whiskey on your breath
Could make a small boy dizzy;
But I hung on like death:
Such waltzing was not easy.

We romped until the pans
Slid from the kitchen shelf;
My mother's countenance
Could not unfrown itself.

27   The hand that held my wrist
Was battered on one knuckle;
At every step you missed
My right ear scraped a buckle.

You beat time on my head
With a palm caked hard by dirt,
Then waltzed me off to bed
Still clinging to your shirt.

THEODORE ROETHKE

Still another method used to suggest multi-dimensional meaning is allusion. In this case, the poet uses familiar historical, literary, or mythical references to communicate his meaning. These references have, in effect, become synonymous with the events themselves and with the values a culture has attached to those events over the years; thus by merely referring to an incident, individual, place, or event, the author suggests all those qualities incorporated into or associated with it. Earlier, Dylan Thomas communicated with freshness, the beauty, the innocence of the Garden of Eden when describing the farm and the morning:

> And then to awake, and the farm, like a wanderer white
> With the dew, come back, the cock on his shoulder; it was all
> Shining, it was Adam and maiden . . .

Note also how, in "Leda and the Swan," W. B. Yeats economically evokes for the reader the violence, beauty, and history of the Age of Heroes by alluding to the violent mythological incidents and characters that gave birth to that cycle of classic civilization. Leda, queen of Sparta, was raped by Zeus, who had descended to her in the form of a swan. The offspring of this union are usually believed to be Pollux and Helen, though two other children borne of Leda, Clytemnestra and Castor, are also sometimes included in this litter. Helen eventually becomes the celebrated cause of the Trojar War, and Clytemnestra becomes the wife of Agamemnon, commander of the Greeks, whom she murders for having sacrificed their daughter, Iphigenia, to appease the gods so that he might insure a safe voyage to Troy for his army.

Leda and the Swan

A sudden blow: the great wings beating still
Above the staggering girl, her thighs caressed
By the dark webs, her nape caught in his bill,
He holds her helpless breast upon his breast.

How can those terrified vague fingers push
The feathered glory from her loosening thighs?
And how can body, laid in that white rush,
But feel the strange heart beating where it lies?

A shudder in the loins engenders there
And Agamemnon dead.
                Being so caught up,
So mastered by the brute blood of the air,
Did she put on his knowledge with his power
Before the indifferent beak could let her drop?

                             W. B. YEATS

Examine the poems which follow and determine where the poet uses allusion and to what he is alluding. Some of the allusions are quite obvious while others are somewhat more subtle and indirect. If the more subtle allusions are unclear, do not hesitate to research them, making use of such resources as the Bible, Greek or Roman myths, and various histories.

Poetry

The Holy Innocents

Listen, the hay-bells tinkle as the cart
Wavers on rubber tires along the tar
And cindered ice below the burlap mill
And ale-wife run. The oxen drool and start
In wonder at the fenders of a car,
And blunder hugely up St. Peter's hill.
These are the undefiled by woman—their
Sorrow is not the sorrow of this world:
King Herod shrieking vengeance at the curled
Up knees of Jesus choking in the air,

A king of speechless clods and infants. Still
The world out-Herods Herod; and the year,
The nineteen-hundred forty-fifth of grace,
Lumbers with losses up the clinkered hill
Of our purgation; and the oxen near
The worn foundations of their resting-place,
The holy manger where their bed is corn
And holly torn for Christmas. If they die,
As Jesus, in the harness, who will mourn?
Lamb of the shepherds, Child, how still you lie.

ROBERT LOWELL

30 chanson innocent

in Just-
spring   when the world is mud-
luscious the little
lame balloonman

whistles   far   and wee

and eddieandbill come
running from marbles and
piracies and it's
spring

when the world is puddle-wonderful

the queer
old balloonman whistles
far   and   wee
and bettyandisbel come dancing

from hop-scotch and jump-rope and

it's
spring
and
     the

          goat-footed

balloonMan   whistles
far
and
wee

                                   e. e. cummings

In California

Here I am, troubling the dream coast
With my New York face,
Bearing among the realtors
And tennis-players my dark preoccupation.

There once was an epical clatter—
Voices and banjos, Tennessee, Ohio,
Rising like incense in the sight of heaven.
Today, there is an angel in the gate.

Lie back, Walt Whitman,
There, on the fabulous raft with the King and the Duke!
For the white row of the Marina
Faces the Rock. Turn round the wagons here.

Lie back! We cannot bear
The stars any more, those infinite spaces.
Let the realtors divide the mountain,
For they have already subdivided the valley.

Rectangular city blocks astonished
Herodotus in Babylon,
Cortez in Tenochtitlan,
And here's the same old city-planner, death.

We cannot turn or stay.
For though we sleep, and let the reins fall slack,
The great cloud-wagons move
Outward still, dreaming of a Pacific.

LOUIS SIMPSON

Hyperbole is overstatement, exaggeration of facts or situa-
tions. A poet may use hyperbole to emphasize a serious point,

32   to achieve a humorous effect, or just to give greater impact
to the poem as a whole. A tour de force achieved primarily
through hyperbole is Karl Shapiro's "The Fly."

The FLY

O hideous little bat, the size of snot,
With polyhedral eye and shabby clothes,
To populate the stinking cat you walk
The promontory of the dead man's nose,
Climb with the fine leg of a Duncan Phyfe
    The smoking mountains of my food
        And in a comic mood
    In mid-air take to bed a wife.

Riding and riding with your filth of hair
On gluey foot or wing, forever coy,
Hot from the compost and green sweet decay,
Sounding your buzzer like an urchin toy—
You dot all whiteness with diminutive stool,
    In the tight belly of the dead
        Burrow with hungry head
    And inlay maggots like a jewel.

At your approach the great horse stomps and paws
Bringing the hurricane of his heavy tail;
Shod in disease you dare to kiss my hand
Which sweeps against you like an angry flail;
Still you return, return, trusting your wing
    To draw you from the hunter's reach
        That learns to kill to teach
    Disorder to the tinier thing.

3
My peace is your disaster. For your death
Children like spiders cup their pretty hands
And wives resort to chemistry of war.
In fens of sticky paper and quicksands
You glue yourself to death. Where you are stuck
    You struggle hideously and beg
        You amputate your leg
    Imbedded in the amber muck.

But I, a man, must swat you with my hate,
Slap you across the air and crush your flight,
Must mangle with my shoe and smear your blood,
Expose your little guts pasty and white,
Knock your head sidewise like a drunkard's hat,
    Pin your wings under like a crow's,
        Tear off your flimsy clothes
    And beat you as one beats a rat.

Then like Gargantua I stride among
The corpses strewn like raisins in the dust,
The broken bodies of the narrow dead
That catch the throat with fingers of disgust.
I sweep. One gyrates like a top and falls
    And stunned, stone blind, and deaf
        Buzzes its frightful F
    And dies between three cannibals.

                              KARL SHAPIRO

In this poem the fly becomes disgustingly grotesque because
Shapiro exaggerates its repulsive characteristics and habits.
Such words as "hideous," "snot," "stinking," "compost,"
"green sweet decay," "stool," "maggots," all emphasize the
filth, the disease with which the fly is associated, an emphasis
so extensive as to create an overwhelming sense of revulsion
in the reader, an emotion far stronger than that ordinarily
felt toward such an innocuous subject.

34   Obviously, exaggeration of this sort does not mean a stretching of the point or even lying. When a poet describes a fly as climbing "with the fine leg of a Duncan Phyfe," or maybe even railroad tracks "stretching to infinity," we realize it is not literally true, though *he is presenting exactly what he sees.* In any case, the purpose of hyperbole is to insure a certain effect through exaggeration—whether the desired effect is to make something more convincing, more aesthetic, to evoke a response or merely to present a striking image.

The literal antithesis of hyperbole is understatement. This occurs when the poet says *less than* he means. He "plays down" the verbal expression of an idea so that what he means is of much greater significance than what he says. The poem's very objectivity, its statement of fact, barren of emotion, works to emphasize the need for human involvement in the situation being described. In "Mending Wall" (page 98) when Frost describes the repair work as "Oh, just another kind of outdoor game,/One on a side. It comes to little more: "—he is understating a task which, in reality, serves to bring neighbors closer together. The tone and the words of this passage serve to understate the act in which the poet and his neighbor are really engaged. It can be seen, therefore, that in hyperbole and understatement, though literally antithetical, the poet uses devices both of which serve to emphasize the truths of his poem.

Notice now how hyperbole and understatement are used in the following poems. Does each poet's approach to his subject add emotional dimension to his point? What is unique about Nemerov's poem that is lacking in each of the other two? Does this difference make the other poems any less effective? How might a poet's use of hyperbole and understatement influence the reader's attitude toward the subjects thus presented? In "Out, Out—" the factual statement at a boy's death underscores the greater significance of the scene.

No one believed. They listened at his heart
Little—less-nothing!—and that ended it.

Poetry

"Out, Out—"

The buzz saw snarled and rattled in the yard
And made dust and dropped stove-length sticks of wood,
Sweet-scented stuff when the breeze drew across it.
And from there those that lifted eyes could count
Five mountain ranges one behind the other
Under the sunset far into Vermont.
And the saw snarled and rattled, snarled and rattled.
As it ran light, or had to bear a load.
And nothing happened: day was all but done.
Call it a day, I wish they might have said
To please the boy by giving him the half hour
That a boy counts so much when saved from work.
His sister stood beside them in her apron
To tell them "Supper." At the word, the saw,
As if to prove saws knew what supper meant,
Leaped out at the boy's hand, or seemed to leap—
He must have given the hand. However it was,
Neither refused the meeting. But the hand!
The boy's first outcry was a rueful laugh,
As he swung toward them holding up the hand,
Half in appeal, but half as if to keep
The life from spilling. Then the boy saw all—
Since he was old enough to know, big boy

36 Doing a man's work, though a child at heart—
He was all spoiled. "Don't let him cut my hand off—
The doctor, when he comes. Don't let him, sister!"
So. But the hand was gone already.
The doctor put him in the dark of ether.
He lay and puffed his lips out with his breath.
And then—the watcher at his pulse took fright.
No one believed. They listened at his heart.
Little—less—nothing—and that ended it.
No more to build on there. And they, since they
Were not the one dead, turned to their affairs.

ROBERT FROST

The Pasture

I'm going out to clean the pasture spring;
I'll only stop to rake the leaves away
(And wait to watch the water clear, I may):
I sha'n't be gone long.—You come too.

I'm going out to fetch the little calf
That's standing by the mother. It's so young,
It totters when she licks it with her tongue.
I sha'n't be gone long.—You come too.

ROBERT FROST

In Place of a Curse

At the next vacancy for God, if I am elected
I shall forgive last the delicately wounded
who, having been slugged no harder than anyone else,
never got up again, neither to fight back,
nor to finger their jaws in painful admiration.

7

They who are wholly broken, and they in whom
mercy is understanding, I shall embrace at once
and lead to pillows in heaven. But they who are
the meek by trade, baiting the best of their betters
with extortions of a mock-helplessness

I shall take last to love, and never wholly.
Let them all into Heaven—I abolish Hell—
but let it be read over them as they enter:
"Beware the calculations of the meek, who gambled nothing,
gave nothing, and could never receive enough."

JOHN CIARDI

Mousemeal

My son invites me to witness with him
a children's program, a series of cartoons,
on television. Addressing myself to share
his harmless pleasures, I am horrified
by the unbridled violence and hostility
of the imagined world he takes in stride,
where human beings dressed in the skins of mice
are eaten by portcullises and cowcatchers,
digested through the winding corridors
of organs, overshoes, boa constrictors
and locomotive boilers, to be excreted
in waters where shark and squid and abalone
wait to employ their tentacles and jaws.
It seems there is no object in this world
unable to become a gullet with great lonely teeth;
sometimes a set of teeth all by itself
comes clacking over an endless plain
after the moving mouse; and though the mouse
wins in the end, the tail of one cartoon

1

38   is spliced into the mouth of the next, where his
rapid and trivial agony repeats itself
in another form. My son has seen these things
a number of times, and knows what to expect;
he does not seem disturbed or anything more
than mildly amused. Maybe these old cartoons
refer to my childhood and not to his
(The ogres in them wear Mussolini's face),
so that when mice are swallowed by skeletons
or empty suits of armor, when a tribe
of savage Negro mice is put through a wringer
and stacked flat in the cellar, he can take
the objective and critical view, while I
am shaken to see the giant picassoid
parents eating and voiding their little mice
time and again. And when the cheery announcer
cries, "Well, kids, that's the end," my son gets up
obediently and runs outside to play.
I hope he will ride over this world as well,
and that his crudest and most terrifying dreams
will not return with such wide publicity.

                                        HOWARD NEMEROV

Tone may be defined as the author's attitude toward his subject, an attitude which comes through to the reader of the poem. It is the emotional or judgmental coloring of the poem, an implicit aspect of the poem usually sensed or recognized by examining many of the elements of the poem previously discussed. One might say that the tone of a poem is like the tone of voice used in daily communication. Animals which do not understand, and children too young to know the language, are nonetheless able to sense when someone is displeased or pleased with them, when to act and when to stop, when to be heard and when to be silent. All this is communicated to them through the tone of voice used, the attitudinal reflector in speech. To correctly interpret the meaning of a poem, one must grasp its tone, for one often learns more about the truth of what is being said by listening to *how* it is being said than by merely listening to *what* is being said. This fact is, of course, precisely what makes hyperbole and understatement so useful and effective. The understatement in the example from "Mending Wall," implies a meaning in terms of the whole poem that is opposite to the one the poem explicitly gives.

This kind of tonal quality is called ironic, or irony. It is ironic that something so important to the human condition as communication between men should be described in such in significant terms as "Oh, just another kind of outdoor game . . ." Perhaps the clearest explanation of irony, in its different forms, is presented by Laurence Perrine in his book *Sound and Sense*. Mr. Perrine recognizes three kinds of irony: dramatic irony, irony of situation, and verbal irony. The particular kind of irony described in "Mending Wall" is dramatic irony, which arises from a contradiction between what the characters in the poem say or do and what the author means. This kind of dramatic irony differs from that which is associated with the theatre. Still another example of dramatic irony appears earlier in the same Frost poem when the neighbor says "Good fences make good neighbors." In both instances, the irony serves to comment indirectly on the author's contradictory intention or meaning, an intention which takes clearer shape as the poem progresses. In addition, this kind of ironic presentation frequently serves to show us the natures of the characters participating in the work, a factor which aids the reader immensely in his judgment of what is being said and what is really meant.

Irony of Situation exists when there is a contradiction between what actually occurs and what is normal to a situation. It is, in effect, an irony of action—the action that occurs is opposite to what is normally expected. Robert Graves' "Call It a Good Marriage" is an excellent illustration of this kind of irony.

40 Call It a Good Marriage

Call it a good marriage—
For no one ever questioned
Her warmth, his masculinity,
Their interlocking views;
Except one stray graphologist
Who frowned in speculation
At her h's and her s's,
His p's and w's.

Though few would still subscribe
To the monogamic axiom
That strife below the hip-bones
Need not estrange the heart,
Call it a good marriage:
More drew those two together,
Despite a lack of children,
Than pulled them apart.

Call it a good marriage:
They never fought in public,
They acted circumspectly
And faced the world with pride;
Thus the hazards of their love-bed
Were none of our damned business—
Till as jurymen we sat on
Two deaths by suicide.

ROBERT GRAVES

In this poem, the poet describes a marriage that, on the sur-
face at least, seems to be a rather normal, mature, well-ordered
relationship. The behavior described in each stanza becomes
shockingly ironic, however, with the disclosure made in the
last two lines.

THE LANGUAGE OF POETRY

Verbal irony occurs when there is a contradiction between what a character says and what he actually means. When the speaker in the Dylan Thomas poem "Do Not Go Gentle Into That Good Night" admonishes his listener to ". . . not go gentle into that good night/rage, rage, against the dying of the light." he is being deliberately verbally ironic in his reference to Death as "good night." If he really meant it to be a *good* night, why should he charge his listener to "rage, rage" against it? By referring to Death as "good night,' he is saying the opposite of what he means.

It is verbal irony that is frequently employed for satire. Satire is a ridiculing, a burlesquing, a "poking fun at" some issue or mode of behavior for the purpose of bringing about correction. It is this intention which distinguishes satire from mere caustic commentary. The satirist makes his point ironically—saying the opposite of what he means, but in a manner that will enable the intelligent reader to see the truth behind the words. The most common kind of satire is that which reduces its target to an extreme degree of the ridiculous. e. e. cummings' poem "next to of course god" is the kind of satiric treatment of the political speaker.

next to of course god

"next to of course god america i
love you land of the pilgrims' and so forth oh
say can you see by the dawn's early my
country 'tis of centuries come and go
and are no more what of it we should worry
in every language even deafanddumb
thy sons acclaim your glorious name by gorry
by jingo by gee by gosh by gum
why talk of beauty what could be more beaut-
iful than these heroic happy dead

who rushed like lions to the roaring slaughter
they did not stop to think they died instead
then shall the voice of liberty be mute?"

He spoke.   And drank rapidly a glass of water

e. e. cummings

Almost the entire poem is composed of the stock clichés, mumbo-jumbo, political chestnuts, and nonsense rambling which are liberally sprinkled throughout innumerable patriotic orations. Throughout the speech, for that is what it obviously is, the speaker reiterates his love for his country "next to of course god." And yet, the reader who accepts this as truth on the speaker's part is missing the insincerity, the glibness, the vacuousness which the poet has so carefully caricatured. It is not love of country that is being satirized but, rather, *how* this love is often expressed. The condemnation, therefore, is of the speaker, who condemns himself through what he is saying. Cummings' point is that too many politicians don't take their own utterances very seriously.

Satire in verse is primarily an exercise of the intellect. Because of this, the satirist always runs the risk of being taken literally and thereby being misunderstood in the extreme. The satirist who is thus misread is accepted as an advocate of the very things he seeks to correct or abolish. He depends as much on the intelligence of his audience for understanding as he does on his own intelligence. It is, in part, this challenge to one's intelligence that makes satire, especially the more subtle kinds, so pleasurable, so delightful to read. Today in a world where new instances of human folly are splashed across the front pages of newspapers everyday, the opportunities for satire, as well as the available talent to take advantage of them, have brought satire to new heights of popularity and influence. Its popularity and effectiveness

43   are evident in the success of such journalists as Art Hoppe and Art Buchwald; such cartoonists as Ron Cobb and Jules Feiffer; such entertainers as Dick Gregory, Godfrey Cambridge, Tom Lehrer; such poets as e. e. cummings, Howard Nemerov, Allen Ginsberg and Lawrence Ferlinghetti. All find vast quantities of material in the issues of war, civil rights, politics, religion, and mechanization.

Some contemporary poetic examples of ironic wit follow. Each of the poems depends on irony for its artistic and communicative success. Consider the poems carefully to determine what kinds of irony are employed and to evaluate how irony contributes to an understanding of the poet's view of the subject he is examining.

Poetry

The Pioneers

The Pioneers had
The best of this country
The boy said.
They grabbed all the
Adventure, Indian-fighting,
                danger
Since, it's been Dullsville.
And he rushed out to his car
And tore down the road
Doing sixty, maybe
And came around a curve
Behind an old Pontiac
Carrying two Barona Indians
Slow-moving, twenty thereabouts.
Overloaded from a scavenging
Trip to the dump.
And the fine pipe for fences
They were taking to the
                reservation
Pierced the boy's skull,
Removing a scalp-lock, neatly

45

And they buried them both, the
            boy
Inside the stockaded Mem'ry
            Garden
And over the fence, in
Joe Booth's car dump
His faithful Mustang.

CHARLOTTE MORTIMER

The Death of the Ball Turret Gunner

From my mother's sleep I fell into the State,
And I hunched in its belly till my wet fur froze.
Six miles from earth, loosed from its dream of life,
I woke to black flak and the nightmare fighters.
When I died they washed me out of the turret with a hose.

RANDALL JARRELL

a man who had fallen among thieves

a man who had fallen among thieves
lay by the roadside on his back
dressed in fifteenthrate ideas
wearing a round jeer for a hat

fate per a somewhat more than less
emancipated evening
had in return for consciousness
endowed him with a changeless grin

whereon a dozen staunch and leal
citizens did graze at pause

46   then fired by hypercivic zeal
             sought newer pastures or because

             swaddled with a frozen brook
             of pinkest vomit out of eyes
             which noticed nobody he looked
             as if he did not care to rise

             one hand did nothing on the vest
             its wideflung friend clenched weakly dirt
             while the mute trouserfly confessed
             a button solemnly inert.

             Brushing from whom the stiffened puke
             i put him all into my arms
             and staggered banged with terror through
             a million billion trillion stars

                                              e. e. cummings

The Dover Bitch
A Criticism of Life

So there stood Matthew Arnold and this girl
With the cliffs of England crumbling away behind them,
And he said to her, "Try to be true to me,
And I'll do the same for you, for things are bad
All over, etc., etc."
Well now, I knew this girl. It's true she had read
Sophocles in a fairly good translation
And caught that bitter allusion to the sea,
But all the time he was talking she had in mind
The notion of what his whiskers would feel like
On the back of her neck. She told me later on

47   That after a while she got to looking out
At the lights across the channel, and really felt sad,
Thinking of all the wine and enormous beds
And blandishments in French and the perfumes.
And then she got really angry. To have been brought
All the way down from London, and then be addressed
As a sort of mournful cosmic last resort
Is really tough on a girl, and she was pretty.
Anyway, she watched him pace the room
And finger his watch-chain and seem to sweat a bit,
And then she said one or two unprintable things.
But you mustn't judge her by that. What I mean to say is,
She's really all right. I still see her once in a while
And she always treats me right. We have a drink
And I give her a good time, and perhaps it's a year
Before I see her again, but there she is.
Running to fat, but dependable as they come.
And sometimes I bring her a bottle of *Nuit d'Amour*.

ANTHONY HECHT

The Lifeguard

In a stable of boats I lie still,
From all sleeping children hidden.
The leap of a fish from its shadow
Makes the whole lake instantly tremble.
With my foot on the water, I feel
The moon outside

Take on the utmost of its power.
I rise and go out through the boats.
I set my broad sole upon silver,
On the skin of the sky, on the moonlight,
Stepping outward from earth onto water
In quest of the miracle

48   This village of children believed
That I could perform as I dived
For one who had sunk from my sight.
I saw his cropped haircut go under.
I leapt, and my steep body flashed
Once, in the sun.

Dark drew all the light from my eyes.
Like a man who explores his death
By the pull of his slow-moving shoulders,
I hung head down in the cold,
Wide-eyed, contained, and alone
Among the weeds,

And my fingertips turned into stone
From clutching immovable blackness.
Time after time I leapt upward
Exploding in breath, and fell back
From the change in the children's faces
At my defeat.

Beneath them I swam to the boathouse
With only my life in my arms
To wait for the lake to shine back
At the risen moon with such power
That my steps on the light of the ripples
Might be sustained.

Beneath me is nothing but brightness
Like the ghost of a snowfield in summer.
As I move toward the center of the lake,
Which is also the center of the moon,
I am thinking of how I may be
The savior of one

Who has already died in my care.
The dark trees fade from around me.

The moon's dust hovers together.
I call softly out, and the child's
Voice answers through blinding water.
Patiently, slowly,

He rises, dilating to break
The surface of stone with his forehead.
He is one I do not remember
Having ever seen in his life.
The ground I stand on is trembling
Upon his smile.

I wash the black mud from my hands.
On a light given off by the grave
I kneel in the quick of the moon
At the heart of a distant forest
And hold in my arms a child
Of water, water, water.

JAMES DICKEY

Boom!

SEES BOOM IN RELIGION, TOO

Atlantic City, June 23, 1957 (AP).—President Eisenhower's pastor said
tonight that Americans are living in a period of "unprecedented re-
ligious activity" caused partially by paid vacations, the eight-hour day
and modern conveniences.

"These fruits of material progress," said the Rev. Edward L. R. Elson
of the National Presbyterian Church, Washington, "have provided the
leisure, the energy, and the means for a level of human and spiritual
values never before reached."

Here at the Vespasian-Carlton, it's just one
religious activity after another; the sky
is constantly being crossed by cruciform
airplanes, in which nobody disbelieves

50   for a second, and the tide, the tide
of spiritual progress and prosperity
miraculously keeps rising, to a level
never before attained. The churches are full,
the beaches are full, and the filling-stations
are full, God's great ocean is full
of paid vacationers praying an eight-hour day
to the human and spiritual values, the fruits,
the means for the level, the unprecedented level,
the leisure, the energy, and the means, Lord,
and the modern conveniences, which also are full.
Never before, O Lord, have the prayers and praises
from belfry and phonebooth, from ballpark and barbecue
the sacrifices, so endlessly ascended.
It was not thus when Job in Palestine
sat in the dust and cried, cried bitterly;
when Damien kissed the lepers on their wounds
it was not thus; it was not thus
when Francis worked a fourteen-hour day
strictly for the birds; when Dante took
a week's vacation without pay and it rained
part of the time, O Lord, it was not thus.

But now the gears mesh and the tires burn
and the ice chatters in the shaker and the priest
in the pulpit, and Thy Name, O Lord,
is kept before the public, while the fruits
ripen and religion booms and the level rises
and every modern convenience runneth over,
that it may never be with us at it hath been
with Athens and Karnak and Nagasaki,
nor Thy sun for one instant refrain from shining
on the rainbow Buick by the breezeway
or the Chris Craft with the uplift life raft;
that we may continue to be the just folks we are,
plain people with ordinary superliners and

51   disposable diaperliners, people of the stop'n'shop
'n'pray as you go, of hotel, motel, boatel,
the humble pilgrims of no deposit no return
and please adjust thy clothing, who will give to Thee,
if Thee will keep us going, our annual
Miss Universe, for Thy Name's Sake, Amen.

HOWARD NEMEROV

Santa Claus

Somewhere on his travels the strange Child
Picked up with this overstuffed confidence man,
Affection's inverted thief, who climbs at night
Down chimneys, into dreams, with this world's goods.
Bringing all the benevolence of money,
He teaches the innocent to want, thus keeps
Our fat world rolling. His prescribed costume,
White flannel beard, red belly of cotton waste,
Conceals the thinness of essential hunger,
An appetite that feeds on satisfaction;
Or, pregnant with possessions, he brings forth
Vanity and the void. His name itself
Is corrupted, and even Saint Nicholas, in his turn,
Gives off a faint and reminiscent stench,
The merest soupçon, of brimstone and the pit.

Now, at the season when the Child is born
To suffer for the world, suffer the world,
His bloated Other, jovial satellite
And sycophant, makes his appearance also
In a glitter of goodies, in a rock candy glare.
Played at the better stores by bums, for money,
This annual savior of the economy

Speaks in the parables of the dollar sign:
Suffer the little children to come to Him.

At Easter, he's anonymous again,
Just one of the crowd lunching on Calvary.

HOWARD NEMEROV

At the beginning of this chapter it was suggested that the inexperienced reader of poetry is often discouraged not only by the language he encounters but also by the physical structure of the genre. When he reads a poem, he is faced with a unit of language that is visually unfamiliar. The words don't stretch across the width of the page; at times, the length of the lines are so irregular as to be disconcerting; the stanzaic patterns do not always seem to fit what he knows about paragraphs; and the rules of grammar and punctuation frequently seem to be governed by the whim of the writer. In short, it doesn't look like prose.

And it isn't prose—but at the same time, it should not be considered so different from prose as to cause the confusion and distress it sometimes does. The principal distinction between the physical nature of poetry and that of prose is based on the rhythm of each—both are rhythmic but poetry is more rhythmically regular than prose. It is not necessary to define rhythm at this point—dancing, tapping a foot to music, or even listening to a heartbeat, are rhythmic experiences common to most people. The insistence on regularity of rhythm is what most often determines the physical nature of a poem. Different rhythms, regularly maintained throughout a poem, result in different poetic structures.

The rhythms of English and American poetry are determined by the occurrence of accented syllables in a line. The rhythm most natural to the English language is *iambic*. In the iambic line, alternate accented and unaccented syllables occur, beginning with the unaccented or unstressed syllable. For example:

```
x  /  x  /  x  /  x  /  x  /
I shot/my friend/to save/my coun/try's life
  x   /  x  /  x  /  x  /   x  /
And when/the hap/py bul/let struck/him dead
```

The reverse of the iambic line is the *trochaic* line. In this case, you still have alternate stressed and unstressed syllables but the order of appearance of each is reversed; in the trochee, the stressed syllable appears first.

```
 /   x   /   x   /   x
Down hill/through this/meadow
```

The *anapest* and *dactyl* rhythms may be considered extensions of the previous two metrical patterns respectively. Anapestic meter is composed of two unaccented and one accented syllable, in that order.

```
 x   x  /   x   x  /  x  x  /
Where the sha/dows are real/ly the bod/y
```

The dactylic, on the other hand, consists of one accented syllable followed by two unaccented.

```
 / x x   /  x  x  / x  x
Orators/follow the/universe
```

Of course, it is possible to combine any number of these different metrical patterns in a single poem, and this is usually the case. A poem of any length with no variety of rhythm can become very monotonous and boring. Such combinations, however, need not make the metrical pattern irregular. In these cases, if regularity of metrical pattern is desired, it is

54   usually retained by a consistent repetition of the various
metrical combinations. This is precisely what e. e. cummings
does in "if everything happens that can't be done."

```
x  /  x x   /   x x  /  x  /
if eve/rything hap/pens that can't/be done
  x  / x x   /  x
(and an/ything's right/er
  x    /
than books/
  x    /
could plan/)
 x /  x x  /  x x  /  x  /
the stu/pidest teach/er will al/most guess
  x  x / xx
(with a run      [CAESURA—See Glossary]
  /
skip/
x /   x x /
around/we go yes/)
   x   /  x x /  x  x /
there's noth/ing as some/thing as one
```

one hasn't a why or because or although
(and buds know better
than books
don't grow)
one's anything old being everything new
(with a what
which
around we come who)
one's everyanything so

so world is a leaf so tree is a bough
(and birds sing sweeter
than books
tell how)
so here is away and so your is a my

(with a down
up around again fly)
forever was never till now

now i love you and you love me
(and books are shuter
than books
can be)
and deep in the high that does nothing but fall

(with a shout
each
around we go all)
there's somebody calling who's we

we're anything brighter than even the sun
(we're everything greater
than books
might mean)
we're everyanything more than believe
(with a spin
leap alive we're alive)
we're wonderful one times one

e. e. cummings

The process one engages in to determine the metrical pattern of a poem is called scansion. A poem is scanned to determine the basic "beat" patterns of the lines as well as the number of times the beat patterns appear per line. This latter aspect is called counting the number of *feet* in each line and is graphically represented in the example above by the slashes between the various syllable combinations. A single foot line is called a monometer line, a two-foot line is dimeter, a three-foot line is trimeter, a four-foot line is tetrameter, a five-foot line is pentameter, a six-foot line is hexameter, and a seven-foot line is heptameter. One infrequently encounters a line of poetry that is longer than seven feet, for the language does

56   not lend itself very easily to lines of this or greater length. Consequently, when one describes the rhythmic pattern of a line of verse, he does so in terms of both the accentuation of

```
                              x  /  x  /
```

syllables and feet; i.e., the iambic illustration I shot/my friend/ . . . would be more completed described as "iambic pentam-

```
                        x  x  /   x   x
```

eter," while the anapestic example where the sha/dows are

```
/   x  x   /  x
```

real/ly the bod/y is "anapestic trimeter." When the rhythmical pattern of a poem is mixed, or contains different, less commonly used syllabic patterns or feet, as in the example

```
x  /  x  x   /  x   x  /  x  /
```

if ev/erything hap/pens that can't/be done, a more detailed explanation of its metrics is usually required. (See Glossary p. 225)

The metrical pattern of a poem frequently reflects and thereby reinforces the content, the attitude, or the tone of the poem. One can easily see how, in cummings' poem, the anapestic quality of the meter, with its bouncy and playful rhythm common to limericks and children's ditties, effectively serves to present a verse describing the frolic, fancy, and joyful innocence of youth. In fact, it is the rhythm more than any other single characteristic of this poem that first and most obviously indicates the nature of the content to the reader. The rhythm skips, pirouettes child-like from line to line and leaps from stanza to stanza, until with a final shouting, "spin/leap/alive we're alive," it bursts free of the limitations of book knowledge into the breathless ecstasy of experimental discovery.

Just as easily recognizable is the influence of the trochaic beat, with its relatively slow and measured step, in the presentation of theme and tone in this stanza from W. H. Auden's "In Memory of W. B. Yeats:"

```
    /  x   /  x   /  x    /
Earth re/ceive an/honored/guest;
```

```
        /  x    /  x    /  x   /
     William/Yeats is/laid to/rest:
        /  x   /  x     /  x    /
     Let the/Irish/vessel/lie
        /  x     /  x   /  x  /
     Emptied/of its/poet/ry.
```

The melancholy tone, appropriate to the subject matter, is echoed in the dirge-like rhythm of the stanza. In this particular case, the funeral rhythm itself is reinforced with an extra, single, accented syllable closing each line of verse.

There is a rhythmic scheme which is more prevalent today than any of the others just discussed—*free verse*. This is verse which follows no systematized metrical pattern, but is rhythmic nonetheless. Whereas the conventional rhythms previously described may exist independent of specific subject matter (they may all be applied to any subject) and are usually brought into play after the tone and theme have been determined, free verse rhythm is unique to the poem of which it is a part; the rhythm emerges naturally out of the content and attitude of the individual poem. In other words, the rhythms of free verse are not imposed upon the content but are rather *inherent* in the material they express and consequently rise out of that material. If handled effectively, this approach allows for a variety of rhythmic structures which frequently enable the poet to move beyond the limitations he encounters within the more traditional, less free-form metrical patterns. A truly fine example of what can be achieved with free verse is Lawrence Ferlinghetti's "Constantly risking absurdity" on page 75. Here, the rhythmical arrangement or accent pattern evolves from the nature of the subject matter. The accent pattern becomes self-defining as soon as the reader realizes that the poem is the "tightrope" described within it, the means by which the poet attempts to cross over to "truth" and "Beauty." As soon as this becomes apparent, the reader finds himself rhythmically moving through the verse like a high-wire acrobat carried along by the "teeter-

58 totter" effect achieved by the unbalanced and irregularly placed lines. This effect forces the eye to jerk quickly back and forth and back again (through not quite so far), then a few quick words (or steps) forward again. The suddenness with which some lines, such as the second one "and death," appear and end to move the reader abruptly, jerkily, on to the next longer and somewhat slower line; the almost complete omission of punctuation, an omission which allows the reader to move constantly, without pause, through the poem, adjusting his rhythm to the language and the scene of the moment until he approaches the end of his journey where the period awaits him—just as the tightrope walker must constantly move, tilt and stagger, constantly adjusting his weight to the wire, coming to rest only when he reaches the platform at the end of the tightrope—are all qualities of the verse form itself which enable the writer to rhythmically emphasize the precariousness, the danger involved in the acrobat's and, metaphorically, in the poet's task.

In some instances, sound patterns (combinations of repeated sounds) influence the rhythmic nature of a verse as much as accent patterns (combinations of repeated stressed syllables) do. Such particular sound patterns as alliteration and onomatopoeia add rhythmic emphasis to a line of poetry, and at the same time they indicate where that emphasis is to be prolonged or where it is to be dramatically curt. An illustration of this principle is, again, "Constantly risking absurdity."

Ferlinghetti makes full use of the explosiveness of certain alliterative words. Alliteration takes place whenever consonants that appear at the beginning of words are repeated—for example, when the poet describes himself as the super-realist "who must *perforce perceive/taut truth/*before the taking of each *stance* or *step.*" The tension of the tightrope journey bursts from such breath expelling words as "perforce perceive" and "taut truth," the explosiveness of the latter being added to by the fact that they join together into a par-

59   ticular kind of forceful poetic foot, the *spondee* / ′′ /—two
accented syllables independent of the debilitating influence of
any unstressed syllable. Immediately following these explo-
sive expressions, the reader is given a series of phrases which
slows him down to a prolonged gliding movement, a move-
ment which imitates the relatively smoother movement of the
acrobat as he nears his goal; in the sibilant sound of "each
stance or step/in his supposed advance/toward the still higher
perch/where Beauty stands and waits," one hears the sound
of soft-soled slippers sliding along the slick wire to the plat-
form. When the sense of the words is suggested in this way,
the effect is called by their sound onomatopoeia. The total
effect of the particular rhythmic structure of Ferlinghetti's
poem is apparent; the reader has not merely been told about
one particular aspect in the experience of being a poet—he
has been allowed to know it, to feel it.

In this section the five basic metrical patterns one might
encounter in English or American poetry have been discussed
so that, hopefully, one should be able to recognize them and
their function in the poems in this or in any other collection.
Any variants of rhythms should offer little difficulty, for they
will all be related to those rhythmic schemes that have been
discussed here. One's knowledge of that discussion may be
tested by examining and scanning the poems that follow.

Poetry

Reasons for Attendance

The trumpet's voice, loud and authoritative,
Draws me a moment to the lighted glass
To watch the dancers—all under twenty-five—
Shifting intently, face to flushed face,
Solemnly on the beat of happiness.

—Or so I fancy, sensing the smoke and sweat,
The wonderful feel of girls. Why be out here?
But then, why be in there? Sex, yes, but what
Is sex? Surely, to think the lion's share
Of happiness is found by couples—sheer

Inaccuracy, as far as I'm concerned.
What calls me is that lifted, rough-tongued bell
(Art, if you like) whose individual sound
Insists I too am individual.
It speaks; I hear; others may hear as well,

But not for me, nor I for them; and so
With happiness. Therefore I stay outside,
Believing this; and they maul to and fro,
Believing that; and both are satisfied,
If no one has misjudged himself. Or lied.

PHILIP LARKIN

Our City Is Guarded by Automatic Rockets

1

Breaking every law except the one
for Go, rolling its porpoise way, the rocket
staggers on its course; its feelers lock
a stranglehold ahead; and—rocking—finders
whispering "Target, Target," back and forth,
relocating all its meaning in the dark,
it freezes on the final stage. I know
that lift and pour, the flick out of the sky
and then the power. Power is not enough.

2

Bough touching bough, touching . . . till the shore,
a lake, an undecided river, and a lake again
saddling the divide: a world that won't be wise
and let alone, but instead is found outside
by little channels, linked by chance, not stern;
and then when once we're sure we hear a guide
it fades away toward the opposite end of the road
from home—the world goes wrong in order to have revenge.
Our lives are an amnesty given us.

3

There is a place behind our hill so real
it makes me turn my head, no matter. There
in the last thicket lies the cornered cat
saved by its claws, now ready to spend
all there is left of the wilderness, embracing
its blood. And that is the way that I will spit

62   life, at the end of any trail where I smell any hunter,
because I think our story should not end—
or go on in the dark with nobody listening.

WILLIAM STAFFORD

Essential Beauty

In frames as large as rooms that face all ways
And block the ends of streets with giant loaves,
Screen graves with custard, cover slums with praise
Of motor-oil and cuts of salmon, shine
Perpetually these sharply-pictured groves
Of how life should be. High above the gutter
A silver knife sinks into golden butter,
A glass of milk stands in a meadow, and
Well-balanced families, in fine
Midsummer weather, owe their smiles, their cards,
Even their youth, to that small cube each hand
Stretches towards. These, and the deep armchairs
Aligned to cups at bedtime, radiant bars
(Gas or electric), quarter-profile cats
By slippers on warm mats,
Reflect none of the rained-on-streets and squares.

They dominate outdoors, Rather, they rise
Serenely to proclaim pure crust, pure foam,
Pure coldness to our live imperfect eyes
That stare beyond this world, where nothing's made
As new or washed quite clean, seeking the home
All such inhabit. There, dark raftered pubs
Are filled with white-clothed ones from tennis-clubs,
And the boy puking his heart out in the Gents
Just missed them, as the pensioner paid

63   A halfpenny more for Granny Graveclothes' Tea
To taste old age, and dying smokers sense
Walking towards them through some dappled park
As if on water that unfocused she
No match lit up, nor drag ever brought near,
Who now stands newly clear,
Smiling, and recognising and going dark.

PHILIP LARKIN

In My Craft or Sullen Art

In my craft or sullen art
Exercised in the still night
When only the moon rages
And the lovers lie abed
With all their griefs in their arms,
I labour by singing light
Not for ambition or bread
Or the strut and trade of charms
On the ivory stages
But for the common wages
Of their most secret heart.

Not for the proud man apart
From the raging moon I write
On these spindrift pages
Nor for the towering dead
With their nightingales and psalms
But for the lovers, their arms
Round the griefs of the ages,
Who pay no praise or wages
Nor heed my craft or art.

DYLAN THOMAS

64   anyone lived in a pretty how town

anyone lived in a pretty how town
(with up so floating many bells down)
spring summer autumn winter
he sang his didn't he danced his did.

Women and men(both little and small)
cared for anyone not at all
they sowed their isn't they reaped their same
sun moon stars rain

children guessed(but only a few
and down they forgot as up their grew
autumn winter spring summer)
that noone lover him more by more

when by now and tree by leaf
she laughed his joy she cried his grief
bird by snow and stir by still
anyone's any was all to her

someones married their everyones
laughed their cryings and did their dance
(sleep wake hope and then)they
said their nevers they slept their dream

stars rain sun moon
(and only the snow can begin to explain
how children are apt to forget to remember
with up so floating many bells down)

one day anyone died i guess
(and noone stooped to kiss his face)
busy folk buried them side by side
little by little and was by was

all by all and deep by deep
and more by more they dream their sleep
noone and anyone earth by april
wish by spirit and if by yes.

Women and men(both dong and ding)
summer autumn winter spring
reaped their sowing and went their came
sun moon stars rain

e. e. cummings

In a Prominent Bar
in Secaucus One Day

To the tune of "The Old Orange Flute"
or the tune of "Sweet Betsy from Pike'

In a prominent bar in Secaucus one day
Rose a lady in skunk with a topheavy sway,
Raised a knobby red finger—all turned from their beer—
While with eyes bright as snowcrust she sang high and clear:

"Now who of you'd think from an eyeload of me
That I once was a lady as proud as could be?
Oh I'd never sit down by a tumbledown drunk
If it wasn't, my dears, for the high cost of junk.

"All the gents used to swear that the white of my calf
Beat the down of the swan by a length and a half.
In the kerchief of linen I caught to my nose
Ah, there never fell snot, but a little gold rose.

"I had seven gold teeth and a toothpick of gold,
My Virginia cheroot was a leaf of it rolled
And I'd light it each time with a thousand in cash—
Why the bums used to fight if I flicked them an ash.

66   "Once the toast of the Biltmore, the belle of the Taft,
I would drink bottle beer at the Drake, never draft,
And dine at the Astor on Salisbury steak
With a clean tablecloth for each bite I did take.

"In a car like the Roxy I'd roll to the track,
A steel-guitar trio, a bar in the back,
And the wheels made no noise, they turned over so fast,
Still it took you ten minutes to see me go past.

"When the horses bowed down to me that I might choose,
I bet on them all, for I hated to lose.
Now I'm saddled each night for my butter and eggs
And the broken threads race down the backs of my legs.

"Let you hold in mind, girls, that your beauty must pass
Like a lovely white clover that rusts with its grass.
Keep your bottoms off barstools and marry you young
Or be left—an old barrel with many a bung.

"For when time takes you out for a spin in his car
You'll be hard-pressed to stop him from going too far
And be left by the roadside, for all your good deeds,
Two toadstools for tits and a face full of weeds."

All the house raised a cheer, but the man at the bar
Made a phonecall and up pulled a red patrol car
And she blew us a kiss as they copped her away
From that prominent bar in Secaucus, N.J.

                                              X. J. KENNEDY

The Now Voices might as well be speechless if they speak
a language incomprehensible to their readers. But the incom-
prehensibility of any language can be easily overcome, if the
individual so desires, by first learning the basic characteristics
of that tongue and then setting about to practice it, to use it.

7   It is in the practice of the language that one puts the finishing
touches on one's ability to understand it. This chapter has
provided the first part of that learning process; now it is up
to the reader to pursue the latter. Nothing will enable the
reader to do this any easier or any better than wide reading
in the vernacular, and what better place to begin applying
one's knowledge of the language of poetry than to the poems
which compose this volume. After all, these people are speak-
ing to us of our time, of our world, and of our place within
it. It is important that we hear them—it is still more important
that we understand them.

Supplementary Poems:

For comparison and discussion

Imagery

Eve of St. Agnes—John Keats
Kubla Khan—Samuel Taylor Coleridge
Poem in October—Dylan Thomas

Simile

I Wandered Lonely As A Cloud—William Wordsworth
The Ecstasy—John Donne
God's Grandeur—Gerard Manley Hopkins

Metaphor

The Yachts—William Carlos Williams
Shall I compare thee to a summer's day (Sonnet 18)—
    William Shakespeare

Symbol

Palladium—Matthew Arnold
Corinna's Going A-Maying—Robert Herrick

Personification

Because I could not stop for Death—Emily Dickinson
To Brooklyn Bridge—Hart Crane

68 *Synecdoche-Metonymy*

The World Is Too Much With Us—William Wordsworth
The Collar—George Herbert

Allusion

Il Penseroso—John Milton
L'Allegro—John Milton

Hyperbole

Valediction: Forbidding Mourning—John Donne
To His Coy Mistress—Andrew Marvell

Understatement

Does It Matter—Sigfried Sassoon
Richard Cory—Edward Arlington Robinson

Irony

The Bishop Orders His Tomb—Robert Browning (Irony of
    Situation)
Ozymandias—Percy Bysshe Shelley (Irony of Situation)
Lovesong of J. Alfred Prufrock—T. S. Eliot (Dramatic Irony)
Andrea del Sarto—Robert Browning (Dramatic Irony)
The Unknown Citizen—W. H. Auden (Verbal Irony)
Base Details—Sigfried Sassoon (Verbal Irony)
Mac Flecknoe—John Dryden (Satire)
The Nymph's Reply to the Shepherd—Sir Walter Raleigh (Satire)

Metrics

Any sonnet (Iambic)
Cargoes—John Masefield (Trochaic)
The Raven—Edgar Allen Poe (Trochaic)
Annabel Lee—Edgar Allen Poe (Anapestic)
Evangeline—Henry Wadsworth Longfellow (Dactylic)
Break, Break, Break—Alfred Lord Tennyson (Spondaic)
The Snake—D. H. Lawrence (Free Verse)

Sound Patterns

The Congo—Vachel Lindsay
Upon Julia's Clothes—Robert Herrick
Sweeney Among the Nightingales—T. S. Eliot
Ode to Evening—William Collins
O Where Are You Going—W. H. Auden

COMMUNI-
CATIONS

INTRODUCTION

The complex nature of today's society is most clearly reflected in the complexity of communication within that society. In an age which has witnessed the development of some of the most sophisticated means of communication known to man—television, telephone, teletype, satellites—it has become increasingly more difficult for man to communicate with his fellow man. This breakdown in communications is a phenomenon which seems to be occurring at all levels of society, from within that smallest of social units, the family, to confusion within international alliances; between teenager and parent as well as between student and teacher; between races within a nation as well as between races of different nations; sometimes, even between members of the same race within the same nation. Throughout the world today, there are countless examples of people speaking with, bargaining with, arguing with, but not communicating with—understanding—each other.

70   This condition permeates almost every aspect of our modern society, but it is especially prevalent in the sciences and in the newspapers. Science, probably the greatest single influence in our society today, is an excellent illustration of the general condition in communications. Ironically, that which has created for us advanced means of communications has itself evolved to the point where it is frequently non-communicative, both to the layman and the scientist. Science has advanced to such a degree in the last twenty years that today the individual is forced to *specialize,* to limit himself to a relatively small portion of the overall scheme of things in order to be able to at least cope with, if not add to, the fund of knowledge already available within a specific discipline.

This specialization reaches such proportions that one frequently finds the available language unequal to the task of describing what is taking place within the discipline; consequently, it becomes necessary to create new terms, new phrases, new "language." This "language" often becomes so particular to the discipline that scientists not only cannot communicate with the layman but, even more significantly, they cannot communicate in many cases with other scientists across scientific disciplines. Thus, from the necessity for specialization in science evolves a specialization of language which, in turn, fosters at least one aspect of the problem of non-communication.

And, this problem of non-communication is not peculiar to the most theoretical or abstract fields of human endeavor. One need only count the number of times in a day he makes decisions on the basis of his lack of understanding of a subject rather than on the basis of informed understanding to realize how uncommunicative he is with the specialist in the field. For example, most people do not communicate with the automobile mechanic who repairs their car. When he starts talking about "manifolds," "headers," "camshaft," "compression checks," "armatures," most people respond with a blank stare and a "Whatever it is, fix it." Nor do they communicate with the appliance salesman who talks about the washing machine in terms of "four-cycle," and "self-lubricating bearing system." One soon realizes that we live in a society which, because of its complexity, is communicatively compartmentalized—a society wherein there exist islands of communication, isolated from each other by the straits of specialization which not only separate the individual from those with whom he may have little in common but from his peers as well.

Actually, to say that the professional does not communicate *at all* with people outside his specialty is not entirely correct. Often there is a kind of understanding, at the most superficial level, between professional and laity which manifests itself in the evolution of another communication "smokescreen" peculiar to our age—*jargon.* Jargon often occurs when certain terms and phrases peculiar to specific disciplines are used by persons who have pretensions to explain, analyze, and discuss almost any situation, regardless of whether or not the terms logically and/or precisely apply to the particular situation. The most flagrant examples of this kind of "communication" may be found in reckless applications of the terminology of psychology. This particular jargon is becoming so thoroughly ingrained in our speech that even people who have, at best, a vague understanding toss about such terms as *Freudian, psychosomatic, neuroses, psychoses, complex (Oedipal, inferiority,* and any other that may be currently in vogue) as if they really knew what they were talking about. The result is a form of non-communication that may be called mis-communication, a condition arising from the misuse of rather specialized terminology to fulfill purposes for which it was never intended.

We have been speaking up to this point, of a very basic kind of noncommunication, one resulting from the specialized demands of a precision-oriented society. But there is presently taking place another, more subtle, more insidious kind of communication corruption. There is a growing tendency in the world today to "dehumanize," "depersonalize" communications, to remove from the communiqué that which gives it value—its significance in terms of the human element, the

72   human involvement of feelings, emotions, beliefs, values. In our newspapers, for example, battles, accidents, disasters, are described in such vagaries as "casualties were described as light (or medium, or heavy), "the victims of one car were identified as Mr. and Mrs. John Smith of San Diego," or "damages were estimated at $2,000,000." This impersonal approach makes it difficult to realize that there are *people* involved in these events, people undergoing despair, pain, torment, fear, and in some cases, even death. The facts are reported objectively, statistically, dispassionately, with a sense of detachment from the experience being witnessed. And one of the consequences of this kind of communication, this kind of objectivity, is that the reader remains uninvolved, detached, incapable of grasping the fact being reported in terms of its significance to him as a human being, an integral part of the human condition. He merely "knows" (records) the fact but does not, cannot, relate to the significance it has for him as a human being. The result on his part is apathy, disinterest, ignorance, and an inability to "communicate" with other people. For before we can communicate, we must "know," that is, understand in its totality that which is being communicated; but we cannot know, the objectivists notwithstanding, what we cannot feel, for feeling is part of that totality. Do we know, *really know*, that a world-wide conflict involving atomic power must inevitably result in the annihilation of such centers of population as New York, Los Angeles, London, Moscow, without at least emotionally imagining, if only for a brief moment, what this knowing would feel like? Can we "know" the experimentation on and the execution of 6,000,000 people at Auschwitz, Buchenwald, and Dauchau by merely recording in our mind's eye the fact, the number, the places, without feeling in our live emotions their significance for us who are part of the human family which both perpetrated and suffered this horror? Can we know what racial oppression and persecution is by merely reading about the vigilante execution in Mississippi of three civil rights workers, two whites and a Negro, without sensing at our core the loneliness, the fear, the pain, the agony, suffered that night on

73   that dark and barren stretch of road near the clay pits.[1] The fact of the matter is that in our society today, we have access to a tremendous amount of facts, but we have lost, or are losing, our human ability to feel them. The inevitable consequence of this condition is that we have lost, or are losing, our ability to communicate with each other.

In some cases, no doubt, the objectivity is as it should be. After all, journalism is concerned with events and the fact of those events, and accepts the responsibility of getting those facts before the people. Very often this accomplishment alone is achieved in the face of such adversity that it is itself a testimonial to journalism's sense of commitment, sense of involvement in the "human condition." But even in journalism it is recognized that the greatest communication is that which assembles the events of the world in such fashion as to make sense as human experience—not as detached, sterile data. What has happened, in most cases, however, is that though we are provided with more facts and knowledge than any previous generation, we do not necessarily communicate with each other any more effectively—sometimes even less effectively—than we did before.

There is, on the other hand, one area of communication which has yet to divorce "knowing" from "feeling"—poetry. Whereas journalism and science are objectively, impersonally concerned with events, poetry is concerned with emotions. To quote Archibald MacLeish, "Journalism wishes to tell what it is that has happened everywhere as though the same things had happened for every man. Poetry wishes to say what it is like for any man to be himself in the presence of a particular occurrence as though only he were there." For the poet is not concerned with dispassionately conveying fact by simply *telling* about an incident—he tries to recreate the *experience* of the fact in order that his reader may know it for himself firsthand. And this is how great poetry functions as an instrument of knowledge—by presenting knowledge with a sense of immediacy for the individual and carrying that knowledge directly to the heart as well as to the mind—by creating an emotional as well as an intellectual experience. It is the poet's

74   purpose not to separate the "knowing" from the "feeling" but to try to capture the *totality* of his experience, both the "knowing" (fact) and the "feeling" (associated emotions), and to crystallize this experience, so to speak, in order that his readers may know it in its totality whenever they read it. It is this desire to "crystallize" the emotional experience which T. S. Eliot is referring to when he speaks of the "objective correlative," a set of objects, a situation, a chain of events which are the formula of a particular emotion; so that when the external facts, which must terminate in the sensory experience, are given, the emotion is immediately evoked. It is this evocation of the emotional experience which Dylan Thomas is referring to when he passionately says:

> What does it matter what poetry *is*, after all? If you want a definition of poetry, say: "Poetry is what makes me laugh or cry or yawn, what makes my toenails twinkle, what makes me want to do this or that or nothing," and let it go at that. All that matters about poetry is the enjoyment of it, however tragic it may be. All that matters is the eternal movement behind it, the vast undercurrent of human grief, folly, pretension, exaltation, or ignorance, however unlofty the intention of the poem.
>
>   —Notes on the Art of Poetry

In a world in which the movement of society seems to be toward compartmentalization and specialization, toward impersonalization and isolation, it is the poet who seeks to burst, emotionally and intellectually, through the communication vacuum and speak to all men. Do we hear him? Listen to the poems that follow.

---

[1] Note: Three young civil rights workers—Andrew Goodman, Mickey Schwerner, James Chaney—disappeared outside Philadelphia, Mississippi, on the night of June 21, 1964. Their bodies were discovered six weeks later in the clay near a den construction site. They had been shot, and Chaney, the Negro, had been savagely beaten as well.

Poetry

Constantly risking absurdity

Constantly risking absurdity
                  and death
    whenever he performs
             above the heads
                  of his audience
  the poet like an acrobat
          climbs on rime
            to a high wire of his own making
and balancing on eyebeams
             above a sea of faces
     paces his way
          to the other side of day
   performing entrechats
          and sleight-of-foot- tricks
and other high theatrics
          and all without mistaking
     any thing
         for what it may not be
  For he's the super realist
          who must perforce perceive
    taut truth

before the taking of each stance or step
in his supposed advance
toward that still higher perch
where Beauty stands and waits
with gravity
to start her death-defying leap
And he
a little charleychaplin man
who may or may not catch
her fair eternal form
spreadeagled in the empty air
of existence

LAWRENCE FERLINGHETTI

Radar

Distance is swept by the smooth
Rotations of power, whose staring
Feelers multiply our eyes for us,
Mark objects' range and bearing.

Linked to them, guns rehearse
Calculated obedience; echoes of light
Trigger the shadowing needle, determine
The flaring arrest of night.

Control is remote: feelings, like hands,
Gloved by space. Responsibility is shared, too:
And destroying the enemy by radar,
we cannot see what we do.

ALAN ROSS

The Printed Word

Distance, with its commensurate decrease of emotional involvement, may be a function of space. But there is another kind of distance, that created by language, which may be even more destructive of feeling. In the following groups of poems, one may see how language can be communicative or non-communicative, depending upon how it is used or not used.

Elderly Nobody Erases Self In Central Park

At three o'clock yesterday afternoon, Jason Quidnunc
An unemployed clock-winder, was observed to be
Walking in Central Park with a large pistol
Dangling from his right hand.   Seventy-three

Years long the dim and twisting way that led
Him to this summer place that had no green
For him.   *The passer-by who happened to notice*
The pistol summoned Patrolman Flaccus O'Flynn.

Distant childhood in Ohio had little warned,
He saw, of that grave darkling fight of a man
Against all men for every scrap of good.
When Quidnunc caught sight of the approaching patrolman,

78   *With a rapid movement he directed the muzzle of the gun*
Against his chest, and fired. At Mercy Hospital
(This small white bed was rentless, which was as well,
For of all he'd lost and gained, zero was total),

He died within the hour.   In "faraway
India" there were four pyramided classes—
Under all, a fifth not tolerable to the rest:
Such is, of course, the inscrutable East and its masses.

Grandpa, your sigh will be an icy knife
Which slices lifeless that black bloom despair,
And all your falling blood be seeds of fire
That snap the flesh of *Ubermensch* and germ
    the vine that will Man's joyful
    scarlet blossom bear.

                                                E. S. FORGOTSON

The following is the complete news release on the bombing
of Nagasaki, August 9, 1945.

> Guam—The second atomic bomb dropped on Japan oblit-
> erated Nagasaki in an inferno of smoke and flame that swirled
> more than 10 miles into the stratosphere and could be seen for
> 250 miles, an Okinawa dispatch said today.
> Flyers told the United Press at Okinawa that the explosion
> was "too tremendous to believe."
> One said that the blinding glare of the blast was so great
> that when it faded he thought for a moment the sun was
> setting.

A later release, that of August 22, was as follows:

> San Francisco—Japanese broadcasters today said atomic
> bomb raids on the cities of Hiroshima and Nagasaki had cost
> nearly half a million "casualties and sufferers" and leveled
> buildings within a radius up to ten miles.

Radio Tokio, in broadcasts recorded by United Press, said effects of the bomb were "monstrous."

The second atomic bomb dropped August 9 on Nagasaki took a toll of "more than 10,000 killed, more than 20,000 wounded, and more than 90,000 rendered homeless in the city," Tokio said.

"Furthermore, many persons are dying daily from burns sustained during the raid," a Tokio propaganda broadcast said.

It followed a few hours after a technical report by Sutezo Torii, technician for Japanese general headquarters, who said it was impossible to obtain shelter within the bombs' effective range.

More than 60,000 were killed at Hiroshima, August 6, Tokio said, and "the number of dead are mounting, as many of those that received burns cannot survive their wounds because of the effects the atomic bomb produced on the human body.

"Even those who receive minor burns," one broadcast asserted, "looked quite healthy at first, only to weaken after a few days from some unknown reason and frequently die."

A Song about Major Eatherly

The book (Fernard Gigon's *Formula for Death—The Atom Bombs and After*) also describes how Major Claude R. Eatherly, pilot of the aircraft which carried the second bomb to Nagasaki, later started having nightmares. His wife is quoted as saying: "He often jumps up in the middle of the night and screams out in an inhuman voice which makes me feel ill: 'Release it, release it.' "

Major Eatherly began to suffer brief periods of madness, says Gigon. The doctors diagnosed extreme nervous depression, and Eatherly was awarded a pension of 237 dollars a month.

This he appears to have regarded "as a premium for murder, as a payment for what had been done to the two Japanese cities." He never touched the money, and took to petty thievery, for which he was committed to Fort Worth prison.

Report in *The Observer*, August 1958.

80   I

Good news. It seems he loved them after all.
His orders were to fry their bones to ash.
He carried up the bomb and let it fall.
And then his orders were to take the cash,

A hero's pension. But he let it lie.
It was in vain to ask him for the cause.
Simply that if he touched it he would die.
He fought his own, and not his country's wars.

His orders told him he was not a man:
An instrument, fine-tempered, clear of stain,
All fears and passions closed up like a fan:
No more volition than his aeroplane.

But now he fought to win his manhood back.
Steep from the sunset of his pain he flew
Against the darkness in that last attack.
It was for love he fought, to make that true.

II

To take life is always to die a little: to stop
any feeling and moving contrivance, however ugly,
unnecessary, or hateful, is to reduce by so much the total
of life there is. And that is to die a little.

To take the life of an enemy is to help him,
a little, towards destroying your own. Indeed, that is why
we hate our enemies: because they force us to kill them.
A murderer hides the dead man in the ground:
but his crime rears up and topples on to the living,

for it is they who now must hunt the murderer,
murder him, and hide him in the ground: it is they
who now feel the touch of death cold in their bones.

Animals hate death. A trapped fox will gnaw
through his own leg: it is so important to live
that he forgives himself the agony,
consenting, for life's sake, to the desperate teeth
grating through bone and pulp, the gasping yelps.

That is the reason the trapper hates the fox.
You think the trapper doesn't hate the fox?
But he does, and the fox can tell how much.
It is not the fox's teeth that grind his bones,
It is the trapper's. It is the trapper, there,
Who keeps his head down, gnawing, hour after hour.

And the people the trapper works for, they are there too,
heads down beside the trap, gnawing away.
Why shouldn't they hate the fox? Their cheeks are smeared
with his rank blood, and on their tongues his bone
being splintered, feels uncomfortably sharp.

So once Major Eatherly hated the Japanese.

III

Hell is a furnace, so the wise men taught.
The punishment for sin is to be broiled.
A glowing coal for every sinful thought.

The heat of God's great furnace ate up sin,
Which whispered up in smoke or fell in ash:
So that each hour a new hour could begin.

82   So fire was holy, though it tortured souls,
The sinners' anguish never ceased, but still
Their sin was burnt from them by shining coals.

Hell fried the criminal but burnt the crime,
Purged where it punished, healed where it destroyed:
It was a stove that warmed the rooms of time.

No man begrudged the flames their appetite.
All were afraid of fire, yet none rebelled.
The wise men taught that hell was just and right.

'The soul desires its necessary dread:
Only among the thorns can patience weave
A bower where the mind can make its bed.'

Even the holy saints whose patient jaws
Chewed bitter rind and hands raised up the dead
Were chestnuts roasted at God's furnace doors.

The wise men passed. The clever men appeared.
They ruled that hell be called a pumpkin face.
They robbed the soul of what it justly feared.

Coal after coal the fires of hell went out.
Their heat no longer warmed the rooms of time,
Which glistened now with fluorescent doubt.

The chilly saints went striding up and down
To warm their blood with useful exercise.
They rolled like conkers through the draughty town.

Those emblematic flames sank down to rest,
But metaphysical fire can not go out:
Men ran from devils they had dispossessed,

And felt within their skulls the dancing heat
No longer stored in God's deep boiler-room.
Fire scorched their temples, frostbite chewed their feet.

The parasitic fire could race and climb
More swiftly than the stately flames of hell.
Its fuel gone, it licked the beams of time.

So time dried out and youngest hearts grew old.
The smoky minutes cracked and broke apart.
The world was roasting but the men were cold.

Now from this pain worse pain was brought to birth,
More hate, more anguish, till at last they cried,
'Release this fire to gnaw the crusty earth:

Make it a flame that's obvious to sight
And let us say we kindled it ourselves,
To split the skulls of men and let in light.

Since death is camped among us, wish him joy,
Invite him to our table and our games.
We cannot judge, but we can still destroy'.

And so the curtains of the mind were drawn.
Men conjured hell a first, a second time:
And Major Eatherly took off at dawn.

IV

Suppose a sea-bird,
its wings stuck down with oil, riding the waves
in no direction, under the storm-clouds, helpless,
lifted for an instant by each moving billow

84

to scan the meaningless horizon, helpless,
helpless, and the storms coming, and its wings dead,
its bird-nature dead:
                        Imagine this castaway,
loved, perhaps, by the Creator, and yet abandoned,
mocked by the flashing scales of the fish beneath it,
who leap, twist, dive, as free of the wide sea
as formerly the bird of the wide sky,
now helpless, starving, a prisoner of the surface,
unable to dive or rise:
                        this is your emblem.
Take away the bird, let it be drowned
in the steep black waves of the storm, let it be broken
against rocks in the morning light, too faint to swim:
take away the bird, but keep the emblem.

It is the emblem of Major Eatherly,
who looked round quickly from the height of each wave,
but saw no land, only the rim of the sky
into which he was not free to rise, or the silver
gleam of the mocking scales of the fish diving
where he was not free to dive.

Men have clung always to emblems,
to tokens of absolution from their sins.
Once it was the scapegoat driven out, bearing
its load of guilt under the empty sky
until its shape was lost, merged in the scrub.

Now we are civilized, there is no wild heath.
Instead of the nimble scapegoat running out
to be lost under the wild and empty sky,
the load of guilt is packed into prison walls,
and men file inward through the heavy doors.

But now that image, too, is obsolete.
The Major entering prison is no scapegoat.

5   His penitence will not take away our guilt,
nor sort with any consoling ritual:
this is penitence for its own sake, beautiful,
uncomprehending, inconsolable, unforeseen.
He is not in prison for his penitence:
it is no outrage to our law that he wakes
with cries of pity on his parching lips.
We do not punish him for cries or nightmares.
We punish him for stealing things from stores.

O, give his pension to the storekeeper.
Tell him it is the price of all our souls.
But do not trouble to unlock the door
and bring the Major out into the sun.
Leave him: it is all one: perhaps his nightmares
grow cooler in the twilight of the prison.
Leave him; if he is sleeping, come away.
But lay a folded paper by his head,
nothing official or embossed, a page
torn from your notebook, and the words in pencil.
Say nothing of love, or thanks, or penitence:
say only 'Eatherly, we have your message.'

JOHN WAIN

The Spoken Word

On the Knowledge of Things

The children tumbling about the yard
Have no moments of awkward hesitation.

Truly growing up is only
Increasing one's awareness

And shaping words
As the slate grows smaller.

What could I say to her
Standing by the bank's wooden railing?

"How are you?" when I know
Her divorce is coming through?

Only awkward words about the weather,
Only smiles, evasions, pleasantries, Damn!

ALEXANDER TAYLOR

⁸⁷ Person to Person

Here they come back again, the harriers,
The worriers, turning the corner,
Always smiling.
Now we will speak, and try to break through.
But there are always the barriers, meaning self,
And the shards of past defeats littering the memory.
Worse than defeat, suppose at our oblique approach
The walls dissolved,
And there self lay as vacant as an O.

    We prefer to go on smiling, and turning away,
Embroidering words into time as slowly as possible,
And never risking such success at all.

LORINE PARKS

Dangling Conversation

It's a still life water color
of a now late afternoon
as the sun shines through the curtain lace
and shadows wash the room
and we sit and drink our coffee
casting our indifference
like shells upon the shore
you can hear the ocean roar
in the dangling conversation
and the superficial sighs
the borders of our lives.

And you read your Emily Dickinson
and I my Robert Frost

88 and we note our place with bookmarkers
that measure what we've lost
like a poem poorly written
we are verses out of rhythm
cuplets out of rhyme
in syncopated time
and the dangling conversation
and the superficial sighs
are the borders of our lives.

Yes, we speak of things that matter
with words that must be said
can analysis be worthwhile
is the theatre really dead
and how the room is softly faded
and I only kiss your shadow
I can not feel your hand
your're a stranger now unto me
lost in the dangling conversation
and the superficial sighs
in the borders of our lives.

                                        PAUL SIMON

Hot Night on Water Street

A hot midsummer night on Water Street—
The boys in jeans were combing their blond hair,
Watching the girls go by on tired feet;
And an old woman with a witch's stare
Cried "Praise the Lord!" She vanished on a bus
With hissing air brakes, like an incubus.

Three hardware stores, a barbershop, a bar,
A movie playing Westerns—where I went
To see a dream of horses called *The Star.* . . .

89   Some day, when this uncertain continent
Is marble, and men ask what was the good
We lived by, dust may whisper "Hollywood."

Then back along the river bank on foot
By moonlight. . . . On the West Virginia side
An owlish train began to huff and hoot;
It seemed to know of something that had died.
I didn't linger—sometimes when I travel
I think I'm being followed by the Devil.

At the newsstand in the lobby, a cigar
Was talkative: "Since I've been in this town
I've seen one likely woman, and a car
As she was crossing Main Street, knocked her down.'
I was a stranger here myself, I said,
And bought the *New York Times*, and went to bed.

LOUIS SIMPSON

Outside of a Small Circle of Friends

Oh look outside the window
There's a woman being grabbed
They've dragged her to the bushes
And now she's being stabbed
Maybe we should call the cops
And try to stop the pain
But Monopoly is so much fun
I'd hate to blow the game
And I'm sure it wouldn't interest anybody
Outside of a small circle of friends.

Riding down the highway
Yes my back is getting stiff
Thirteen cars are piled up

90   They're hanging on a cliff
Now maybe we should pull them back
With our tow and chain
But we've got to move and we might get sued
And it looks like its gonna rain
And I'm sure it wouldn't interest anybody
Outside of a small circle of friends

Sweating in the ghetto
With the colored and the poor
The rats have joined the babies
Who are sleeping on the floor
Now wouldn't it be a riot
If they really blew their tops
But they git too much already
And besides we've got the cops
And I'm sure it wouldn't interest anybody
Outside of a small circle of friends

Oh, there's a dirty paper
Using sex to make a sale
The Supreme Court was so upset
They've sent him off to jail
Maybe we should help the fiend
And take away his fine
But we're busy reading Playboy
And the Sunday New York Times
And I'm sure it wouldn't interest anybody
Outside of a small circle of friends

Smoking marijuana is more fun than drinking beer
But a friend of ours was captured
And they gave him thirty years
Maybe we should raise our voices
Ask somebody why
But demonstrations are a drag
And besides we're much too high

91   And I'm sure it wouldn't interest anybody
Outside of a small circle of friends

Oh look outside the window
There's a woman being grabbed
They've dragged her to the bushes
And now she's being stabbed
Maybe we should call the cops
And try to stop the pain
But Monopoly is so much fun
I'd hate to blow the game
And I'm sure it wouldn't interest anybody
Outside of a small circle of friends

PHIL OCHS

Out of Blindness

Give names to sounds,
if it so please you:
call the abrupt tumultuous thrum
of gasoline explosion—"airplane."
But it is not.
It is noise obliterating bird-song.

Call wind among invisible leaves,
"rustling whisper of the trees."
But it is not.
It is an oval defined by silence,
wherein a multitude
of faint staccato clicks
sound magically.

Say—if you like—the weightless warm
against my cheek is sunlight,
and the cool my cheek feels

92   (penetrating yet leaving undisturbed
the film of warmth) is wind.
I will agree and we will play our game.
But do not ask me to believe
That *name* and *feel* are quite the same.

Your language of the sight is current coin
for our transaction, I agree.
But in my *real*
not seen things count
but sound and what I feel.
I link these, each to each
within the brain until—
thought alien in your world—
my tongue can speak your speech to a degree
that buys me privilege of your company.

LESLIE B. BLADES

Monologue of a Deaf Man

'Et lui comprit trop bien, n'ayant pas entendu.'

—Tristan Corbière

It is a good plan, and began with childhood
As my fortune discovered, only to hear
How much it is necessary to have said.
Oh silence, independent of a stopped ear,
You observe birds, flying, sing with wings instead.

Then do you console yourself? You are consoled
If you are, as all are. So easy a youth
Still unconcerned with the concern of the world
Where, masked and legible, a moment of truth
Manifests what, gagged, a tongue should have told;

93   Still observer of vanity and courage
And of these mirror as well; that is something
More than a sound of violin to assuage
What the human being most dies of: boredom
Which makes hedgebirds clamour in their blackthorn cage.

But did the brushless fox die of eloquence?
No, but talked himself, it seems, into a tale.
The injury, dominated, is an asset;
It is there for domination, that is all.
Else what must faith do deserted by mountains?

Talk to me then, you who have so much to say,
Spectator of the human conversation,
Reader of tongues, examiner of the eye,
And detective of clues in every action,
What could a voice, if you heard it, signify?

The tone speaks less than a twitch and a grimace.
People make to depart, do not say 'Goodbye.'
Decision, indecision, drawn on every face
As if they spoke. But what do they really say?
You are not spared, either, the banalities.

In whatever condition, whole, blind, dumb,
One-legged or leprous, the human being is,
I affirm the human condition is the same,
The heart half broken in ashes and in lies,
But sustained by the immensity of the divine.

Thus I too must praise out of a quiet ear
The great creation to which I owe I am
My grief and my love. O hear me if I cry
Among the din of birds deaf to their acclaim
Involved like them in the not unhearing air.

DAVID WRIGHT

94   Law in the Country of the Cats

When two men meet for the first time in all
Eternity and outright hate each other,
Not as a beggar-man and a rich man,
Not as a cuckold-maker and cuckold,
Not as bully and delicate boy, but
As dog and wolf because their blood before
They are aware has bristled into their hackles,
Because one has clubbed the other to death
With the bottle first broached to toast their transaction
And swears to God he went helpless black-out
While they were mixing smiles, facts have sacked
The oath of the pious witness who judged all men
As a one humble brotherhood of man.

When two men at first meeting hate each other
Even in passing, without words, in the street,
They are not likely to halt as if remembering
They once met somewhere, where in fact they met,
And discuss "universal brotherhood,"
"Love of humanity and each fellow-man,"
Or "the growing likelihood of perpetual peace,"
But if, by chance, they do meet, so mistaking,
There will be that moment's horrible pause
As each looks into the gulf in the eye of the other,
Then a flash of violent incredible action,
Then one man letting his brains gently to the gutter,
And one man bursting into the police station
Crying: "Let Justice be done. I did it. I."

TED HUGHES

The Dual Site

To my twin who lives in a cruel country
    I wrote a letter at last;
For my bones creaked out in our long silence
    That seven years had passed,

Seven whole years since he and I
    By word or token exchanged
The message I dare not do without:
    That still we are not estranged,

Though I watch figures in a city office
    And he the waves of the sea,
Keeping no count since he hardly cares
    What happens to him or to me;

Since to names and numbers he closed his head
    When, children still, we were parted,
Chose birth and death for his calendar,
    But leaves the dates uncharted,

Being one who forgets what I remember,
    Who knows what I do not,
Who has learnt the ways of otter and raven
    While I've grown polyglot.

Lately I found a cactus in flower
    And feared for his apple-trees,
Dozed in the club and saw his cattle
    Drag with a foul disease,

96   And my bones grown stiff with leaning and lying
                Cried out that I'll labour in vain
        Till I help my twin to rebuild his hovel
                That's open to wind and rain.

        So I sent him a note, expecting no answer,
                And a cheque he'd never cash.
        For I knew he was one who'd smile if he heard
                His own roof come down with a crash,

        But above the porpoise-leaping bay
                Where ploughshare fin and tail
        Cut furrows the foam-flecked sea fills up
                He'd stand in the swishing gale,

        Calm as the jackdaws that nest in crannies
                And no more prone to doubt,
        With gull and cormorant perched on the rocks
                Would wait the weather out.

        Yet he wrote by return: "Have no fear for your dwelling
                Though dry-rot gnaws at the floors;
        Only lighten their load of marble and metal,
                Keep clear the corridors,

        Move out the clocks that clutter your study,
                And the years will leave you alone:
        Every frame I know of lasts long enough,
                Though but cardboard, wood or bone.

        And spare me your nightmares, brother, I beg you,
                They make my daemons laugh,
        They scare the spirits that rarely will visit
                A man with no wand or staff,

        With no symbol, no book and no formula,
                No lore to aid him at all,

Who wherever he walks must find the image
    That holds his mentors in thrall.

But your waking cares put down on paper
    For me to give to the wind,
That the seed may fall and the dry leaf crumble,
    Not a wisp be left behind

Of the tangle that hides the dual site
    Where even you and I
Still may meet again and together build
    One house before we die."

                              MICHAEL HAMBURGER

Love Poem

These words are all of me
    that I may show
        to name you what I am.
For what I am is words,
    and what you are is an
        idea wrapped in syllables.
I'll name you "body" and
    you tremble love
        in warm return.
The form is cool if
    naming's not the flame;
        the form is void.
I'll quote you yesterdays if you
    will speak tomorrows made
        from our todays.
Seek movement with me: for,
    though actions shout, I've merely words
        to name what we might be.

                                  LEWIS TURCO

98 What's in a Word?

What's in a word?
Why, all of man's known nature:
Even the feathered, fluttery, flying, singing thing
Was not a bird
Until man made it to a word.

What's in a word?
Well, Time, with a restless past—
Life, in a restive place—an ungrasped sword
An ever-present shield—
All of tomorrow than can never be concealed.

What's in a word?
What is in a word? Today
All of the debt we each have failed to pay;
A whole completed through the self,
A sudden sky,
Rhythm wind rain pain laughter you—I.

CAROL SHINE

Mending Wall

Something there is that doesn't love a wall,
That sends the frozen-ground-swell under it
And spills the upper boulders in the sun,
And makes gaps even two can pass abreast.
The work of hunters is another thing:
I have come after them and made repair
Where they have left not one stone on a stone,
But they would have the rabbit out of hiding,
To please the yelping dogs. The gaps I mean,

No one has seen them made or heard them made,
But at spring mending-time we find them there.
I let my neighbor know beyond the hill;
And on a day we meet to walk the line
And set the wall between us once again.
We keep the wall between us as we go.
To each the boulders that have fallen to each.
And some are loaves and some so nearly balls
We have to use a spell to make them balance:
"Stay where you are until our backs are turned!"
We wear our fingers rough with handling them.
Oh, just another kind of outdoor game,
One on a side. It comes to little more:
There where it is we do not need the wall:
He is all pine and I am apple orchard.
My apple trees will never get across
And eat the cones under his pines, I tell him.
He only says, "Good fences make good neighbors."
Spring is the mischief in me, and I wonder
If I could put a notion in his head:
"*Why* do they make good neighbors? Isn't it
Where there are cows? But here there are no cows.
Before I built a wall I'd ask to know
What I was walling in or walling out,
And to whom I was like to give offense.
Something there is that doesn't love a wall,
That wants it down." I could say "Elves" to him,
But it's not elves exactly, and I'd rather
He said it for himself. I see him there,
Bringing a stone grasped firmly by the top
In each hand, like an old-stone savage armed.
He moves in darkness as it seems to me,
Not of woods only and the shade of trees.
He will not go behind his father's saying,
And he likes having thought of it so well
He says again, "Good fences make good neighbors."

ROBERT FROST

100 Supplementary Poems:
For comparison and discussion

Auto Wreck
Karl Shapiro

The Hollow Men
T. S. Eliot

Death of the Hired Man
Robert Frost

Dover Beach
Matthew Arnold

The Second Coming
W. B. Yeats

Richard Cory
Edward Arlington Robinson

John Gorham
Edward Arlington Robinson

Essay on Man
Alexander Pope

Effort at Speech Between Two People
Muriel Rukeyser

DISSENT

INTRODUCTION

Dissent has always been a part of the American spirit. Our nation was born of protest against certain unfair practices of the British. The dissent of the people was recorded in history by the angry publishers of the Revolutionary period and is still being expressed by the bitter, angry young poets of today. But protest is not only reflected in written documents. It can take many forms—from the silent refusal to vote or the boycott of a product or a bus to rallies, marches, and finally to violent demonstrations. And in our time, even to the self-immolation of a youth on the steps of a public building. The poet records the fact of the discord within the society not as a chronicler but in terms of the passion, in terms of the depths of feeling, and in terms of the disruption within the society. He records words and sounds, and at times he combines words with music as do some of our contemporary musician poets. As he records, he gives voice to the feelings of dissenters and clarifies for them emotions that they are feeling but are perhaps unable to verbalize. Each individual will choose the avenue of protest which is available to him and which is consistent with his talents and appropriate to his time. Some will choose to march, some to organize groups, some to run for office, some to resist the system with passivity; but the poet, by expressing his dissent through words and images, often speaks to and for the rest of us.

Like poets, students have, through their protests, traditionally promoted growth and change in the institutions of society. Contemporary students, perhaps reflecting the greater discontent and polarization within our society today, are protesting more loudly and with more public response than in any previous period in our history. What is the source of the discontent that is felt within much of society and that is being expressed by young adults? To borrow from Oscar Wilde's definition of a cynic, it may be safe to generalize that today's dissent is against a society that knows the price of everything and the value of nothing.

Some of the major issues raised by youthful dissenters are the shallowness of contemporary values that emphasize materialism; man's inhumanity to his fellow man as exemplified by his willingness to wage war and his inability or refusal to correct racial injustices; and finally the continued, reckless pursuit of an affluent society at the expense of a healthy environment.

Students see their parents and other adult models measuring a man's worthy in terms of his possessions rather than his talents, his degree rather than his knowledge, his job title rather than his productiveness or creativity. They see the educational institution more hospitable to those seeking pieces of paper—in the form of degrees, credentials, certificates—than those seeking information and knowledge; and they question the purpose of education. They see art dealers selling and collecting masterpieces—not because the works are beautiful, provocative, or because art can enrich the owner's existence, but because art is good insurance against inflation. Consequently, they question the value of creative work. They see a society which seeks to accumulate wealth and goods beyond the usefulness of such materials; multi-millionaires stockpiling additional millions are admired, homebuilders adding

03 more and more bathrooms to their plans are considered forward looking; and a nation stockpiling bombs to increase the dimensions of "overkill" is considered prudent. Therefore, they continue to question the values of society.

In a society where bigger means better, they wonder what happens to quality and craftsmanship. The creativity of the individual is removed from his productions and his craft becomes work. He no longer feels a sense of pride and accomplishment; he sits as one of thousands engaged in routine or even automatic occupations, often without an understanding of the relationship between his operation and the eventual goal. Salary replaces job satisfaction as the reason for continued output. As his work loses meaning and intrinsic value, man loses a measure of his own meaning and individual value.

Our society is bombarded daily by the commercial measures of a man. The successful man—the good man—uses deodorant, germicide soap, and mouth fresheners as a courtesy to his friends. As the young uncomfortably apply their deodorants, they suspect that they are being taken, and resent the view that a man is courteous because he smells good. Mr. Ideal looks clean, pressed, and close shaven; he washes often, eats and drinks low-calorie meals, and smokes tobacco with grace, but nothing is said of how he treats his fellow man. Much of society and its poet spokesmen might well question Madison Avenue's propositions about what is worthy in man in order to demonstrate to society that they feel man's essential humanity involves more than external features.

Most of today's students and young poets can look at our society with a newer perspective, freed from the grinding economic responsiblity of their elders. Many of today's young people have been permitted a personal history of prosperity and affluence that has not included the fears and anxieties suffered by their parents during the depression years. From a new and different—even privileged—vantage point these young pople can see the discrepancies and futilities that members of the older generation, busily engaged in maintaining their economic place, do not easily notice.

104   When youth shouts his contempt for what he sees, exaggerates his claims, or acts with equal vulgarity in the opposite direction—as in giving up not only the overvaluation of deodorant but the occasional shower as well—he might well expect some of the righteous anger to be returned by the hardworking man. The man who has worked hard all his life and is still struggling with payments, mortgages and insurance premiums that will provide advantages for his family feels defeated, confused, and bitter when he hears his life condemned. Perhaps both strident and gentle voices need to be raised in unison. To speak to all of America and man's essential humanity, America's youth will need to keep his own humanity foremost.

A new concern for humanity has grown in America during the long years of Vietnam involvement; an increasing number of Americans have begun to look critically at the brutality of war, at the killing, the maiming, and the starving. Many have looked with horror at the effects upon civilians and children who lose homes, families, ways of life, even their reason to live in many instances—and they ask, Why? The new and closer look at war—at the use of military force—grew out of concern over the Vietnam situation, but the new attitudes toward war are not exclusive to the question of Vietnam or its politics. It is rather that involvement in Vietnam marked a time when the realities of war and of blood were viewed in a frame of reference that denied the glamour and romance of former wars.

The voices of students and the "now" poets are among the most forceful and passionate ones raised on this issue. They are the individuals most closely touched by war. They are the ones who are being asked to put their courage, their ideals, and their lives on the line. They are asked to do this, but they are given little voice in the decisions of the nation. Their letters, their outcries, their marches seem to go unheeded by the decision-makers. But still they speak. They are forced to personal choices in the question of honor and perhaps in the question of the entire course of their lives at a time when they are still establishing the value systems by which they will live. Their voices ring with awareness as they speak of Vietnam, of war, of killing their fellow man, and of dying.

It is not only the struggle of nations and governments that fills the young poets with despair, but also the racial brutality on our city streets between races and the callousness of the "haves" for the poverty-stricken and hungry. The poet has seen violent expressions of the anger and fearfulness that continue to widen the gulf between black and white. He sees the senselessness of generations forced to live with second-class status and prejudice that has not been altered by legislation and court decision. He sees the anger and frustration of black youth which on occasion leads to excesses and loud rhetoric. He witnesses with horror the vengeance of mayors, policemen, and citizens who shout "shoot to kill." He sees somber tragedy in the assassination of voices of leadership, sees the national despair and the absurdity of the death of a President, a Senator, a distinguished American Nobel Prize statesman and eminent black leader. The poet voices dissent, he makes us see the injustice, the despair, the rage, the hurt.

The crisis between blacks and whites is most visible, the pain most quickly felt, but the misery of other groups without power in the society is also within the cognizance of the poet. So the plight of the poor from whom society takes much, spends some, does little appears in the poet's verse as well.

The final area of dissent is not unique to contemporary society; it is as old as man's thought, but it finds unique expression and formulation in terms of our times. Man has always recognized certain unfriendly forces in nature, and with the prize of consciousness he was also forced to accept the painful recognition of the inevitability of his own death, the fact of his ultimate frailty. In the past, man has dealt with this question in a variety of ways. He sought to deny nature's unfriendly aspects through scientific and technological control and through "harnessing" the power of nature.

Contemporary man's renewed concern with the very old question of his relationship to the environment has a new dimension. Man is no longer concerned exclusively with the old notion of "pushing back" nature to build a city in the clearing; alarm is now increasingly voiced for the results of man's careless, at times even contemptuous, disregard for the nature he has been "pushing back."

Poets have long reminded us that we have been courting disaster as we ignored the natural world around us in our rush to remake the environment. Now voices are raised in protest against the waste that has been the result of a history of thoughtless use of nature; against pollution of the air and water, against destruction of forests and vegetation, against reckless uses of poisons that hasten the demise of wild species, against the tons of litter and garbage that offend and diminish all of us. Poet protestors now remind us of nature's revenge and ask us to consider the question—as we destroy the environment are we not also destroying man?

Death of the environment, then, is translated more personally into the question of one's own death, a concern that poets have traditionally articulated. Man's attempts to meet the crisis of his own death have led him to religion, to various attempts to escape, and to an increased awareness and affirmation of the value inherent in the struggle of life. Today young poets are reflecting youth's renewed interest in religion in all its aspects as an approach to life. Some of their poetry reflects the protests that are being raised within the church by the young, the poor, and the alienated against outmoded traditions and against unresponsiveness to contemporary issues. And while there is much of confrontation in these protests, the protestors do not deny the role of religion in their lives; they are, rather, demanding more support from religion.

Man has discovered an infinite number of ways to escape consciousness—obsessive work, self-centered pursuits, short cuts to enlightenment, dimmed senses. Poets have protested escapes that rob life of its meaning; for the poet as for the dramatist, it is the struggle against the forces that threaten life that gives meaning to existence. Poets give voice to the notion that we should not only give up the escape of denying death, but we should be consistently aware of the immediacy of death—for only through the awareness of that eventuality will life gain its full meaning. In the poet's view, life lived on the edge of death is more brilliant, more valued, more carefully spent, than life spent in endless, mindless monotony. In this way, it is not really death, but the meaningfulness of life to which they direct attention.

For the alienated, the dangerous, difficult world of to-morrow that cannot be predicted seems hardly worth striving toward. For the escapist, whether through drugs, through diminution of awareness by some other method, or through failure of commitment, it matters little that life is stripped of its meaning and value. But in increasing numbers there are others who state with vision and clarity that in the face of the certainty of uncertainty, in the face of the absurdity of much of our life, it is imperative that we find meaning in our personal existence, that we act, that we speak out with what-ever capability we have about those aspects of our society with which we disagree—even when our voices are lost in the thunder of the storm moving away from us, even when our dissent is lost in the sea of diverse opinions and injustices.

For today's young poets, it is the dissent and the struggle toward just goals—not whether the world hears the dissent, nor even whether goals are attained—it is the dissent and the struggle itself that gives life its meaning and which for them defeats absurdity, lack of power, meaninglessness, even death.

The poems that follow express the concerns of young poets regarding injustice, lost values and lost resources. They claim our attention as dramatically and forcefully as a placard in a demonstration. In the first two poems, written by a boy twelve years old, we learn something more of Martin Luther King, Jr. and the world of small boys than the news reports were able to communicate.

Poetry

war war

war war
why do god's children fight among each other
like animals
a great man once lived
a Negro man
his name was the Rev. Martin Luther King.

but do you know what happened
he was assassinated by a white man.
a man of such knowledge as he
Martin Luther King
a man of such courage
to stand up and let a man hit him
without hitting back

yes—
that's courage
when you fight back of course you're brave
but do you think you yourself can stand up
and let someone beat you

09 without batting an eyelash
that takes courage.

shot him down
that's right
one of god's children

well you can count on a long hot summer
one of our black leaders has been killed
murdered
down into the gutter

I will long remember this dark day.

it's funny it's so you can't
even walk out in the street anymore
some maniac might shoot you
in cold blood.

what kind of a world is this?

I don't know.

MICHAEL GOODE (age 12)

Shot with a Hot Rot Gun

There once was a day when
I used to say
Martin Luther King was nothing.

But a day came when, when
everybody had to eat their words
because he was dead,
shot with a hot rot gun.

MICHAEL GOODE (age 12)

¹¹⁰ Medgar Evers

For Charles Evers

The man whose height his fear improved he
arranged to fear no further. The raw
intoxicated time was time for better birth or
a final death.

Old styles, old tempos, all the engagement of
the day—the sedate, the regulated fray—
the antique light, the Moral rose, old gusts,
tight whistlings from the past, the mothballs
in the Love at last our man forswore.

Medgar Evers annoyed confetti and assorted
brands of businessmen's eyes.

The shows came down: to maxims and surprise.
And palsy.

Roaring no rapt arise-ye to the dead, he
leaned across tomorrow. People said that
he was holding clean globes in his hands.

GWENDOLYN BROOKS

Malcolm X

For Dudley Randall

Original.
Ragged-round.
Rich-robust.

He had the hawk-man's eyes.
We gasped. We saw the maleness.
The maleness raking out and making guttural the air
and pushing us to walls.

And in a soft and fundamental hour
a sorcery devout and vertical
beguiled the world.

He opened us—
who was a key,

who was a man.

GWENDOLYN BROOKS

Foreign Policy Commitments or You Get Into the Catamaran First, Old Buddy

y digamos que, pensamos que, like
it doesn't work, you
talk of the war in vietnam—only you don't—
dear committee, you talk most about ways
of expressing your rage against it, only
you do not say it is rage, too
timid, baby, you are a beast in a trap.
                         fierce but rational
                         (maybe they'll let me out?)
                         You know they won't
and there's the persistent sense of animal rage, to
strike back to strike out
at what hurts you, hurts them too, I mean the reality

112   the children who will grow up to hate us,
the Vietnamese girl blinded and burnt by our napalm and
        still / lives, has lost all her hair, is
        still pregnant
        and will bear the child if we leave any hospitals for them,
not, whatever ditch or ricefield or building still standing,
                that 10 Americans die
that's her only wish

                    I wonder why?
                    here we are saving Southeast Asia, etc.
                    And everyone knows this, every
                    one feels it

                    Bombs fall and are flowers
                    the stamen is the whole village
                    blossoming, the
                    wood and tin and flesh flung outward
                    are petals . Death

                    is beautiful! Mussolini's son-in-law, what
                    was his name, Ciano?   count Ciano
                    has described it accurately . The
                    image is true . That was 1937

How the villages explode under the blossoming bombs!
Lovely! the bodies thrown up like wheat from the threshing
flail?
It sure as hell is poetic and this is 1966 and what shall we
do against it?

The dead horse
nibbles
dead grass

in a dead pasture . There
is no green anywhere, horse,
pasture, grass, it's all
b l a c k .

> Whatsa matter with you?
> Hasn't anyone
> ever seen
> a b l a c k h o r s e ?
>
> PAUL BLACKBURN

The Gift of Fire

*In memory of Norman Morrison, who burned himself to death in front
of the Pentagon on November 2, 1965*

In a time of damnation
when the world needed a Savior,
when the dead gathered routinely,
comic-strip flat and blurred,

he took the god at his promise
and set himself on fire,
skin, brain, sex, smile

so we should see, really see
by that unbearable light
the flower of the single face,
the intricate moth of consciousness:

but he lived in the land of the one-eyed
where the blind is king.

LISEL MUELLER

114 Of Late

"Stephen Smith, University of Iowa sophomore, burned what
    he said was his draft card."
And Norman Morrison, Quaker, of Baltimore Maryland,
    burned what he said was himself.
You, Robert McNamara, burned what you said was a concen-
    tration
of the enemy aggressor.
No news medium troubled to put it in quotes.

And Norman Morrison, Quaker, of Baltimore Maryland,
    burned what he said was himself.
He said it with simple materials such as would be found in
    your kitchen.
In your office you were informed.
Reporters got cracking frantically on the mental disturbance
    angle.
So far nothing turns up.

Norman Morrison, Quaker, of Baltimore Maryland, burned,
    and while burning, screamed.
No tip-off. No release.
Nothing to quote, to manage to put in quotes.
Pity the unaccustomed hesitance of the newspaper editorialists.
Pity the press photographers, not called.

Norman Morrison, Quaker, of Baltimore Maryland, burned
    and was burned and said
all that there is to say in that language.
Twice what is said in yours.
It is a strange sect, Mr. McNamara, under advice to try
the whole of a thought in silence, and to oneself.

GEORGE STARBUCK

Paraders for the Bomb

Full of a nitty-gritty anxiety,
I walk the plank of possible doom around me.
An unruly gust cuts the corner of
Lexington and 60th Street, loosing
a wayward placard around my feet.
The mustard-colored message reads,
"Bomb Hanoi." Three blond toughs, Rover Boys
for the hour, slice in and out of the
Bloomingdale's crowd. On one lapel are
"Drop It" buttons, on the other
"Buckley For Mayor." They made the marching
team, these three parts of the river
of patriotism that swamped Fifth Avenue,
in a tempest of cheers for war in Vietnam.
Darting into the subway, they exhale
a vapor of belligerent righteousness,
as they head back to the neighborhood
of their fears. The shoppers (O dreamers
of the ultimate bargain!) hardly notice
the boutonniered boys. Too busy
with the map of purchasing, they miss
the territory of violence around them.

SIDNEY BERNARD

Norman Morrison

On November 2nd 1965
in the multi-coloured multi-minded
United beautiful States of terrible America
Norman Morrison set himself on fire

116   outside the Pentagon.
He was thirty-one, he was a Quaker.
and his wife (seen weeping in the newsreels)
and his three children
survive him as best they can.
He did it in Washington where everyone could see
because
people were being set on fire
in the dark corners of Vietnam where nobody could see.
Their names, ages, beliefs and loves
are not recorded.

This is what Norman Morrison did.
He poured petrol over himself.
He burned. He suffered.
He died.
That is what he did
in the white heart of Washington
where everyone could see.
He simply burned away his clothes,
his passport, his pink-tinted skin,
put on a new skin of flame
and became
Vietnamese.

ADRIAN MITCHELL

Norman Morrison

Not an unhappy man
but one who could not stand
in the silence of his mind
the cathedral
emptied of its ritual
and sounding about his ears
like a whirlwind.

117   He cradled the child awhile
       then set her down nearby
       and spoke in a tongue of flame
       near the Pentagon
       where they had no doubt.

               Other people's pain
               can turn so easily
               into a kind of play.
               There's beauty
               in the accurate
               trajectory. Death
               conscripts the mind
               with its mysterious
               precision.

                                        DAVID FERGUSON

Leaflets

(For Brian Patten and my twelve students at Bradford)

Outside the plasma supermarket
I stretch out my arm to the shoppers and say:
"Can I give you one of these?"

I give each of them a leaf from a tree.

The first shopper thanks me.
The second puts the leaf in his mack pocket where his wife
     won't see.
The third says she is not interested in leaves. She looks like a
     mutilated willow.
The fourth says: "Is it art?" I say that it is a leaf.
The fifth looks through his leaf and smiles at the light beyond.

118   The sixth hurls down his leaf and stamps it till dark purple
         mud oozes through.
         The seventh says she will press it in her album.
         The eighth complains that it is an oak leaf and says he would
         be on my side if I were also handing out birch leaves, apple
         leaves, privet leaves and larch leaves. I say that it is a leaf.
         The ninth takes the leaf carefully and then, with a backhand
         fling, gives it its freedom.
         It glides, following surprise curving alleys through the air.
         It lands. I pick it up.
         The tenth reads both sides of the leaf twice and then says:
         "Yes, but it doesn't say who we should kill."

But you took your leaf like a kiss.

They tell me that, on Saturdays,
You can be seen in your own city centre
Giving away forest, orchards, jungles.

ADRIAN MITCHELL

The March

(For Dwight Macdonald)

Under the too white marmorial Lincoln Memorial,
the too tall marmorial Washington obelisk,
gazing into the too long reflecting pool,
the reddish trees, the withering autumn sky,
the remorseless, amplified harangues for peace—
lovely, to lock arms, to march absurdly locked
(unlocking to keep my wet glasses from slipping)
to see the cigarette match quaking in my fingers,
then to step off like green Union Army recruits
for the first Bull Run, sped by photographers,
the notables, the whores . . . fear, glory, chaos, rout . . . /

our green army staggered out on the miles-long green fields,
met by the other army, the Martian, the ape, the hero,
his new-fangled rifle, his green, new, steel helmet.

ROBERT LOWELL

The March

Where two or three were heaped together, or fifty,
mostly white-haired, or bald, or women . . . sadly
unfit to follow their dream, I sat in the sunset
shade of their Bastille, their Pentagon,
nursing leg and arch-cramps, my cowardly,
foolhardy heart; and heard, alas, more speeches,
though the words took heart now to show how weak
we were, and right. An MP sergeant kept
repeating. "March slowly through them. Don't even brush
anyone sitting down." They tiptoed through us
in single file, and then their second wave
trampled us flat and back. Health to those who held,
health to the green steel head . . . to the kind hands
that helped me stagger to my feet, and flee.

ROBERT LOWELL

March on the Delta

One more March
unrolls eyeballs
with scald of scenes
that are dues paid
for space to live:
the eagle flies high
over Mobile as the wind
prays in the street

120   and a tear gas fog
washes Selma faces
in oxides of nowhere
as we skip double dutch
in space and show
those Russians while
stars fall on Alabama.

One more March
of whirlyhawks over Mekong
sow a notquitelethal
smog of maggots
on a defoliate scene
where a lone leaf sighs
a final spring
to a listless world

as our face is saved
the fig leaf is gone.

ART BERGER

1965

Here, in the thick Carolina darkness,
I hear the bombers rumbling from Fort Bragg.

Three hundred miles north of here,
in the air stinking with mist off the Potomac,

the President hunches on the White House lawn.
His dogs are with him, and he is weary.

They sniff and nuzzle his rough hunter's hand.

GIBBONS RUARK

1 Night Riders

The massive trembling of late dusk air
Has drawn me from my house on this low hill:
A line of helicopters droning south
Rides one by one on the dark hump
Of eastern woods. More and more coming,
They strut their huge exoskeletal forms
In the waning light, flash
A shifting mathematical sequence
Of pale green lights.
Their rumble disposes all that is left of the day.

An invisible sack, coarse enough to stand alive,
Settles upon me, leaving holes for eyes.
I ride into night on the cover of an old well,
A raft of heavy weathered boards.

JEAN FARLEY

Winter: For An Untenable Situation

Outside it is cold. Inside,
although the fire has gone out
and all the furniture is burnt,
it is much warmer. Oh let
the white refrigerator car
of day go by in glacial thunder:
when it gets dark, and when
the branches of the tree outside
look wet because it is so dark,
oh we will burn the house itself
for warmth, the wet tree too,

122   you will burn me, I will burn you,
and when the last brick of the fireplace
has been cracked for its nut of warmth
and the last bone cracked for its coal
and the andirons themselves sucked cold,
we will move on!, remembering
the burning house, the burning tree,
the burning you, the burning me,
the ashes, the brick-dust, the bitter iron,
and the time when we were warm,
and say, "Those were the good old days."

ALAN DUGAN

The Blackstone Rangers

1 AS SEEN BY DISCIPLINES

There they are.
Thirty at the corner.
Black, raw, ready.
Sores in the city
that do not want to heal.

2 THE LEADERS

Jeff. Gene. Geronimo. And Bop.
They cancel, cure and curry.
Hardly the dupes of the downtown thing
the cold bonbon,
the rhinestone thing. And hardly
in a hurry.
Hardly Belafonte, King,
Black Jesus, Stokley, Malcolm X or Rap.
Bungled trophies.
Their country is a Nation on no map.

3 Jeff, Gene, Geronimo and Bop
in the passionate noon,
in bewitching night
are the detailed men, the copious men.
They curry, cure,
they cancel, cancelled images whose Concerts
are not divine, vivacious; the different tins
are intense last entries; pagan argument;
translation of the night.

The Blackstone bitter bureaus
(bureaucracy is footloose) edit, fuse
unfashionable damnations and descent;
and exulting, monstrous hand on monstrous hand,
construct, strangely, a monstrous pearl or grace.

3 GANG GIRLS

A Rangerette

Gang Girls are sweet exotics.
Mary Ann
uses the nutrients of her orient,
but sometimes sighs for Cities of blue and jewel
beyond her Ranger rim of Cottage Grove.
(Bowery Boys, Disciples, Whip-Birds will
dissolve no margins, stop no savory sanctities.)

Mary is
a rose in a whiskey glass.

Mary's
Februaries shudder and are gone. Aprils
fret frankly, lilac hurries on.
Summer is a hard irregular ridge.
October looks away.
And that's the Year!

Save for her bugle-love.
Save for the bleat of not-obese devotion.

Save for Somebody Terribly Dying, under
the philanthropy of robins. Save for her Ranger
bringing
an amount of rainbow in a string-drawn bag.
"Where did you get the diamond?" Do not ask:
but swallow, straight, the spirals of his flask
and assist him at your zipper; pet his lips
and help him clutch you.

Love's another departure.
Will there be any arrivals, confirmations?
Will there be gleaning?

Mary, the Shakedancer's child
from the rooming-flat, pants carefully, peers at
her laboring lover. . . .
Mary! Mary Ann!
Settle for sandwiches! settle for stocking caps!
for sudden blood, aborted carnival,
the props and niceties of non-loneliness—
the rhymes of Leaning.

GWENDOLYN BROOKS

Going Home

For Mick Jagger

When one billion insurance
adjustors, graduate
assistants in classics, penologists,
neurologists, astronomers

25   and phrenologists threw down their
instruments when the box
sang you, did you smile?
                              Who
couldn't get no
can't get no
                    What
occurs behind that sweet mongoloid
gape? You
live us more, going
nuts for us.
                    Mick, driving
down to LA I saw, last summer, two
nuns, black on a Malibu
doughnut-glazed as the sun
went black, dear God, and they had their
portable . . .
                    Do it, baby, then, go
nuts for us, be most us, help us,
going home.

TIM REYNOLDS

Orpheus

Between two lines of print
a voice is tearing.
Newspaper ink spreads on the tips of my fingers.

I pull towards me, making the fine sound.
It is a falls, a whisper,
a stretch of giving like the shout of a distant crowd.

There is a sharpness to it, a note like fat burning.
Even thinking
gets into it, this stripping between facts.

126   It is the news of a last speech.
Tall women
are running through the high grass towards bloody water.

MICHAEL GOLDMAN

Boy Breaking Glass

To Marc Crawford
from whom the commission

Whose broken window is a cry of art
(success, that winks aware
as elegance, as a treasonable faith)
is raw: is sonic: is old-eyed première.
Our beautiful flaw and terrible ornament.
Our barbarous and metal little man.

"I shall create! If not a note, a hole.
If not an overture, a desecration."

Full of pepper and light
and Salt and night and cargoes.

"Don't go down the plank
if you see there's no extension.
Each to his grief, each to
his loneliness and fidgety revenge.
Nobody knew where I was and now I am no longer there."

The only sanity is a cup of tea.
The music is in minors.

Each one other
is having different weather.

127 "It was you, it was you who threw away my name!
And this is everything I have for me."

Who has not Congress, lobster, love, luau,
the Regency Room, the Statue of Liberty,
runs. A sloppy amalgamation.
A mistake.
A cliff.
A hymn, a snare, and an exceeding sun.

GWENDOLYN BROOKS

To A Red-headed
Do-good Waitress

Every morning I went to her charity and learned
to face the music of her white smile so well
that it infected my black teeth as I escaped,
and those who saw me smiled too and went in
the White Castle, where she is the inviolable lady.

There cripples must be bright, and starvers noble:
no tears, no stomach-cries, but pain made art
to move her powerful red pity toward philanthropy.
So I must wear my objectively stinking poverty
like a millionaire clown's rags and sing, "Oh, I

got plenty o' nuttin'," as if I made
a hundred grand a year like Gershwin, while
I get a breakfast every day from her for two
weeks and nothing else but truth: she has
a policeman and a wrong sonnet in fifteen lines.

ALAN DUGAN

128 Birmingham Sunday*

Come 'round by my side and I'll sing you a song,
I'll sing it so softly it'll do no one wrong,
On Birmingham Sunday the blood ran like wine,
And the choirs kept singing of freedom.

That cold autumn morning O I saw the sun,
And Addie Mae Collins her number was one,
In an old Baptist church there was no need to run,
And the choirs kept singing of freedom.

The clouds they were dark and the autumn winds blew,
And Denise McNair brought the number to two,
The falcon of death was the creature she knew,
And the choirs kept singing of freedom.

The church it was crowded and no one could see,
That Cynthia Wesley's dark number was three,
Her prayers and her feelings would shame you and me,
And the choirs kept singing of freedom.

When young Carol Robertson entered the door,
The number her killers had given was four,
She asked for a blessing and asked for no more,
And the choirs kept singing of freedom.

On Birmingham Sunday a noise shook the ground,
And people all over the earth turned around,

*Editor's note:

One chilly September Sunday morning in 1963, an explosion ripped the
16th Street Baptist Church in Birmingham, Alabama. When the debris
was cleared, four girls ranging in age from 11 to 14 lay dead, the vic-
tims of bigotry and hate.

129 For no one recalled a more cowardly sound,
And the choirs kept singing of freedom.

The men in the forest they once asked of me,
"How many blackberries grow in the blue seas?"
And I asked them right back with a tear in my eye,
"How many dark ships in the forest?"
The Sunday has come, the Sunday has gone,
I can't do much more than sing you a song,
I'll sing it so softly it'll do no one wrong,
And the choirs kept singing of freedom.

RICHARD FARINA

You Get Used to It

*"Am I in Alabama or am I in hell?" A minister,
Montgomery, Alabama, March 1965*

Begging-bowl eyes, begging-bowl eyes,
skin round hoops of wire.
They do not eat, they are being eaten,
saw them in the papers.

But it's only bad if you know it's bad,
fish don't want the sky.
If you've spent all your life in hell or Alabama
you get used to it.

Ignorant husband, ignorant wife,
each afraid of the other one's bomb.
He spends all he has in the Gentlemen's
on a half-crown book of nudes.

But it's only bad if you know it's bad,
fish don't want the sky.

130   If you've spent all your life in hell or Alabama
you get used to it.

Beautiful blossom of napalm
sprouting from the jungle,
bloom full of shrivelling things,
might be mosquitoes, might be men.

But it's only bad if you know it's bad,
fish don't want the sky.
If you've spent all your life in hell or Alabama
you get used to it.

I hurt, you hurt, he hurts, she hurts,
we hurt, you hurt, they hurt.
What can't be cured must go to jail,
whta can't be jailed must die.

But it's only bad if you know it's bad,
fish don't want the sky.
If you've spent all your life in hell or Alabama
you get used to it.

ADRIAN MITCHELL

Testimonies for a School Prayer

Now we are at peaceful war
quickly the child ducks
behind a kneeling cardboard tank
shot up by paper planes

When I grow up
torn from a box-top
I'll build a bomb
to drop on cereal cities

131   Melt my rings
my decoding system
sometime along my 40th yr
I'll grow up—I promise—

Now in fire bombs
there is real fire
even Prometheus
a fool would know that

A village is not made of cardboard
but of dried hay burning
the people are not cut-outs
but peasants beating their bodies

So the flames are real
so the village is real
so the helicopter is real
so I am a cut-out.

SERGE GAVRONSKY

Women in Brooklyn

Women sit on a street in Brooklyn;
The homes of their blood are soft with dust.

Their words unravel as they lean back in their chairs
And hear the ocean several blocks away.

Their dresses hang close to them like flimsy coffins.
Darkness moves at their shoulders,
And their bodies
Are shored up with strange timber.

PAUL ZWEIG

132 Contemporary Fear

In the alley he lay on what was
    once his side
And he prayed for his other arm
    and the rest of his head.
Clutching the machinegun they
    had extruded for him,
He aimed at a clump of oil-covered
    sand, though the barrel
Was bent by a car that had driven
    over not an hour before.

He was like all the rest once—two arms;
    two legs with wide and stable boots; a
Helmet; and (of course) the gun, the inevitable gun;—
    and everything that sick, sad green.
Millions of them, like their big flesh
    brothers, have lost their green arms
And their green legs and, some, their heads;
    but, as he lay there, I thought
The loss was not the same for
    he was Mattel—and maiming's swell.

The real thought was not for the plastic soldier,
    but for the child who left him there.
Did some little warlord find more constructive play?;
    or, as I fear, did he cut off the arms and legs?

DON OBER

19 ? ?

thinking the unthinkable
he concluded that two armies
were safer than one

133   because varied response
meant flexible posture
minimizing the need to risk
preventive first strikes
which was utmost responsibility
in that mushroom mania where
offense is defense
(or as some suggest,
defense is offense)
leaving the single concern
that national prestige
might be tarnished
if he had to incinerate
in order to preserve—
a grievous possibility when
war is peace

DAN GEORGAKAS

On Seeing a Stamp from the Democratic Republic of Vietnam

As a boy I collected stamps
and their rainbows paid passage
beyond city alleys, prairies or factories.
Madagascar, Algeria, Bosnia-Herzegovina, Indo-China.
    Names
yet more than names.
    People
yet more than people.

The years wrinkled from politics
and stamps got pasted to our living skin,
mad as butterflies: Danzig, Poland, the Ukraine,

134   and a letter canceled The Republic of Spain
before brave Germans marched
to obliterate names and people.
But we were young. We waited for stones to bleed.
And days limped by like wounded sheep.

Now America marches,
less brave, perhaps, less honest in its *kampf*,
and Vietnam becomes another stamp to catalog
or cross off the human map.

But can any collector boast
how one stamp of mother and child
sowing rice beneath bombs of Pax Americana
is traded for one celebrating the Wehrmacht?
That stamp sets fire to our books.

LESLIE WOOLF HEDLEY

The Art of Poetry

You can say anything.
That a young marine charging up a sand incline at Saipan
suddenly thought of mittens on a string.
That after hours in the museum
all is quiet; the Rubens in Trafalgar Square,
for example, stay well within their frames.
That the lake of the mind no longer at civil war
must be lovely and quiet, with delightful small fish
nibbling near the surface.
That Rasputin's toenails
must have been clipped by someone:
where are such traces now?
That the impossible sea
is heaving tonight at the flanks
of a ship with lights and music . . .

35   of many ships, carrying an unguessable number
of indiscretions, and not a few smokers
considering the jump.
That a flagpole doesn't care—
how silly to march past it on a fine Tuesday
in a small group dressed the same
and hitting the left feet at approximately the same instant.
That the air above your sleeping son's head
is as holy as rain.

That nothing is perfect: an unpleasant woman
said on television tonight I should think of my stink.
That the next person you turn to
may be the only one you'll ever have a chance
to love more than yourself.
That a statue is not a fiesta.
That the snow makes so little noise.
That a car goes by. Slows down, stops, back up.
Pauses, the motor whirring—and drives off.
It is midnight and October in America.
The small towns are left to the leaves.

DENNIS TRUDELL

In Mexico

Mexican
Flea powder
Hair tonic,
Soap smells.
Silence.
Eight men
In the
Peluqueria Allende
(Barbershop),

136   Reading
Comic books.

La Terraza
10 PM, May Day.
All over
There are riots
America, America:
All I know of it
Are the petitions
I am asked to sign.
Incredible!
What foolishness—
I am convinced,
I sign. I read
Some more,
And I sign.

I am marching
On Washington,
Los Alamos,
The Pentagon,
Chicago,
The State Department.
I am financing ads
In the New York *Times*,
Dark nights
Of the soul.
Rhetoric
Pomposity,
America,
There is nowhere
To go
But to march
On you
March on you—
What a country!
For even

37
Your stupidity,
The charm
Of your
Tastelessness,
Vitality,
Greed

>   *America, get out*
>   *Of Vietnam,*
>   *The Dominican Republic,*
>   *Africa, Europe*
>   *Southeast Asia*

Has begun to smell
Has begun to smell
I would say
Like the Pentagon,
Like senility
Like death.

ROBERT SWARD

I Looked Over Jordan

Underneath were the everlasting arms
Of God, whose features were the future's.

A seamless sea ravelling at its edge
Spun Jordan's thread to the Dead Sea:

At Jericho a wall of standing water
Built without hands or martyr-mortar

Wove with the eye, a familiar marvel
Far from the city of Adam. At Gibeon

The sun and moon like stones in ice
Shone in the neutral light of miracle,

138   The heavenbent bow arrowed with stars
        Hung from noon with unstrung skyline

        In a vision, knotholed in time's grain.
        Like a shawl drawn over the shoulders

        Of children, or a wave woven by shoals
        Of hills, God gathered from the east

        The night's goodly Babylonish garment
        That would fade, rent by falling stars.

LANE DUNLOP

Stability Before Departure

        I have begun my freedom and it hurts.
        Time opens out, so I can see its end
        as the black rock of Mecca up ahead.
        I have cut loose from my bases of support
        and my beasts and burdens are ready, but
        I pace back and forth across my right
        of way, shouting, "Take off! Move out
        in force!", but nothing moves. I wait
        for a following storm to blast me out of here
        because to go there freely is suicide!
        Let the wind bear my responsibility.

ALAN DUGAN

Poem

In the old days either the plaintiff or the defendant won or lost
justly or unjustly according to the mood of the court; the
        innocent

and the guilty were acquitted or condemned according to their
   luck
or pull with justice. Nowadays they are all condemned to death
by hard labor, together with the lawyers, juries, and arresting
   police.
Then the boards of review condemn the presiding judges too,
for having wasted time. In this way, all those who are in any
   way
connected with justice are impartially disconnected, and the
   clerk
closes the court house to join the last judgement. This is not to
   say
that there is no more justice: as an only natural human
   invention to
begin with, it has turned into the needs of the state, which
   needs labor.
The whole apparatus can be forgotten in the absence of
   individuals
to whom to apply it, and the sensible man will have nothing
   to do
with anything outside his inner, passional life except his
   position.

ALAN DUGAN

Supplementary Poems
For comparison and discussion

Dulce Et Decorum Est

Wilfred Owen

On The Late Massacre at Piedmont

John Milton

Advice to a Prophet

Richard Wilbur

THE NOW VOICES

IDENTITY

INTRODUCTION

"What is my purpose in life?" "What is my role in society?" "How am I related to my fellow man?" "Who am I?" These are fundamental questions with which every individual must deal. Many people are preoccupied with these questions for much of their lives; some never really find the answers but they continue to seek self-knowledge.

The search for identity is one of man's basic tasks, and as such it is a point of human contact. Even while isolated in the perceptions and experiences of his own search for identity, each man shares with others a common, though personal, struggle. The poet, in addressing himself to the question of his own identity, illuminates for others the universality of the search.

When the poet speaks of himself as a unique individual, he is expressing his identity by building a picture from countless small things that he does, that he feels, and that others observe about him; all these small things together

142   reveal the unity of his personality. Thus Cruz in "Sometimes on my way back" reveals his identity when he says about himself: "I like to hate too/I like to burn/I like to fight."

An individual's identity is the sense of himself, gained through experience, that forms a thread of recognizable continuity throughout his life as he changes, grows, and develops. He finds his identity in that which is constant about himself as he moves through time and between groups. He looks for the continuity in his relationship to the environment, to society, to work, to loved and valued individuals, to his fellow man, and to God for the answer to the question of who he is. Poets attempt to express and define these relationships for themselves and for others. The new poets also talk about those aspects of modern society that increase man's identity confusion: the growing importance of machines and the constantly shifting order, values, and goals of contemporary society.

As machines take over more and more of his routine jobs, modern man asserts a belief that his human quality makes him different from—implicitly, superior to—the machine. He seeks to demonstrate that his identity contains more than work functions, that he is more than a robot. When a university student struggles against becoming a computer number, he maintains that he has a more real identity that must be preserved. Most people prefer to keep their names as their identity labels rather than the more easily coded Social Security numbers; those who can easily remember addresses, phone numbers, and calendar dates often "forget" their Social Security numbers. Recently, voices have been raised against the telephone company's convenient all-digit dialing; people wanted to retain the exchange names that had become a part of their identity. Man sees numbers, numerical tables, and statistics defining more and more of his life, and he resists, however feebly.

Poets have long confronted machines in their poetry and have discussed the effect of automation on the lives of modern man. More recently poets have been confronted by machines as practitioners of their own art; just as many workers have watched computers usurp their function, poets have seen the computer turn out poetry. This computer poetry experiment is one of the most interesting of the group of experiments in which machines are given tasks that man usually considers part of his intellectual identity; computers play chess, computers are detectives, computers select dates, and now computers are writing poetry. The most notable poet among the machines is RCA 301. This poet produces intriguing, structurally correct, superficially provocactive material. Computer programmers set the form of the poems; they decide the number of words to appear, the number of lines to a poem and the relationship of nouns to adjectives and verbs and adverbs. The computer does the rest. A computer programmed in this way can turn out as many as one hundred and fifty poems per minute. A few examples of poetry by RCA 301 follow.

Poem No. 927

WHILE LIFE REACHED EVILLY THROUGH EMPTY FACES
WHILE SPACE FLOWED SLOWLY O=ER IDLE BODIES
AND STARS FLOWED EVILLY UPON VAST MEN
NO PASSION SMILED

RCA 301

Poem No. 929

WHILE DREAM FLOWED BLINDLY ON BROKEN HOPES
STILL SPACE DRAINED SICKLY O=ER BROKEN LOVES
YOUR LIGHT DRIVEN SLOWLY FROM FURTIVE MEN
NO HEAVENS SLEPT

RCA 301

Poem No. 078

THOUGH STARS DRAINED SICKLY UPON IDLE HOVELS
FOR LIFE BLAZED FAST UPON EMPTY FACES
WHILE BLOOD LOOMED BITTER ON IDLE FIELDS
NO MARTIAN SMILED

RCA 301

Poem No. 105

OUR WATER FLOWED MEANLY AGAINST EMPTY SKIES
OUR BLOOD DYING EVILLY NEAR EMPTY BODIES
AND GLOOM FLOWED MEANLY THROUGH GAUNT
    FACES
OUR FOE PALLED

RCA 301

Poem No. 140

YET LIGHT REACHED BITTER FROM FURTIVE LOVES
YOUR BLOOD DRIVEN FOULLY =NEATH INHUMAN
    HOVELS
FOR STARS DRAINED FREELY =ROUND BLACK DEEDS
THE HEAVENS PALLED

RCA 301

The first response to the 301 poetry is often "how amaz-
ing," and if one makes an effort, he can sometimes find mean-
ing, or what for a moment seems meaningful, in these poems.
But now compare the five works from the 301 with some of

the poems in this section. The human poet will never win a competition with the 301 in terms of gross productivity, but what he does produce, though it takes countless hours instead of hundredths of a second, can achieve a quality of humanity, relevance, and importance far surpassing anything that the 301 can create. The poet can say things about himself and about his world that help us understand ourselves and our world better; 301 lacks the human experience to achieve that end.

The young poets not only tell us about machines, they also illuminate the contemporary stresses resulting from shifting values, changing goals, and the multiple—often conflicting —roles that society presses upon an individual. Faced with a numbered identity, an ever-increasing population, rapid world travel, and mass communication, modern man discovers that many of the old modes of finding his place in society have been destroyed. It is no longer easy for him to find his identity in ancestral family groups, in trade, or even in community groups. As the old order of things is threatened, modern man frequently resorts to the establishment of pseudo-identities by becoming a member of a cult or by participating in a temporary fad. This surrender to instant and prescribed social values, whether anti-establishment or establishment in sentiment, is a failure to create a meaningful personal identity.

What about the special problems of identity faced by individuals who cannot lose themselves in the mass community? What about individuals who seem to be different because they look different, because they are afflicted or handicapped, or because they are members of a minority group? Much of a man's identity grows out of his perception of other people's reactions to him. Countee Cullen, in the poem "Incident," brings this concept into sharp focus. Individuals who find others responding to them primarily in terms of an anomaly or of skin color and only slightly, if at all, in terms of human qualities, will find it difficult to keep this aspect of their identity from assuming an overriding importance.

146   Occasionally a leader, a poet, or a folk hero emerges to show society that it is possible to accept traditional values without overlooking the unique demands of the present. These men help society surge forward in periods of change that require action.

Some of the voices seem new and strange, some are saying important things, some are saying frivolous things. Which ones have the most meaning and importance for our time? Perhaps only future scholars will know which of these men were able to rise as lasting poets, not only because of what they said but because of the import their words had for their fellow man. Some of the poets writing today, including students in the classroom, may be the ones whose words can help adapt the values of a changing social order in a constructive personal way that will help all men find their own meaning and identity.

Poetry

A Week In Paradise

1

A man one out of his head—
he knew it, he kept shaking it—
full of something, but stuck
like salt in a salt-shaker
    in wet weather—
patrolling down State Street,
his hand pointed in every shop window
shaking. Something will have to be done,
this man may be dangerous
    or become dangerous.
His hair shoots out of his head, also
some sort of words like seeds
blown all ways over smooth pavements.
He is observed in Santa Barbara
    in the climate of Paradise.

2

The baseball season is as old as the sycamores:
It is weary and seamed,

148   The pitchers last only three innings,
The batters have all fallen under the low .300s.
The fans in the stands half attending
Tune their excitement elsewhere on small transistors.
Who cares who wins the pennants! They are already won,
In the heavenly register where all statistics sleep.
The sycamore leaves turn brown and harsh,
Their thick brown fingers like ancient fielder's gloves.
Their magic number is five, or seven.

3

The birdbath willows clearly, a reservoir.
Dark watermosses spreading across its bed.
A small wind feathers the top.
The birdbath: the bird-path—
Is there any dividing line?
The high trees hide
A congress of invisible clamor.

4

Pastures and meadows, the wide
walking places of poets,
and the sea-cliffs, sharply edged,
where the air falls down:
these, and the spring wildflowers,
among which the poet forgets
the class structures, falling on
the five-pointed blues

and the mustard-yellows of the spring meadows
falling into his summer poem
as the cold sea collapses:
these are now forgotten

amid the late sharp teeth
of the summer foxtails.

5

Nasturtiums. Isn't the name enough?
They go from fire-yellow to orange-and blood-red
Growing abundant in shade—
With long naked stems, like roots,
The flowers "strangely and refreshingly fragrant."

I went to pick some.
They came off the earth, as if
They lived on the waters of the air,
Transplanted now, they look proper;
If they are not wildflowers, still they belong wild.

6

All day the mountains like black satin
In heaps and folds, without motion.
Now night rises up them out of the gulleys,
Like Wolfe's men up the cliffs of Quebec.
They stir and turn, breathless.
The shadows creep in by the streamhead at Painted Caves.
The stars are moving,
Like bright silver buttons.

7

Confusions of a hard day
Come clear in three breaths.

My barber who cannot stay awake at night,
He even fell asleep on a piano bench!

150   An astrology guide tells me what I knew already
But did not know I knew, in the drugstore.

And now the god-damned dog
Falls into a pit of swamp water.

It all comes clear, as you see,
Water dissolving all troubles.

JOHN RIDLAND

The Family Goldschmitt

Punctual as bad luck,
The aerogramme comes sliding
Under the door, mornings,
Addressed to the Family Goldschmitt.
My landlady puts it there.

My landlady—that blonde aura
Of everything Nordic, Clairol
And kroner, the Dowager Queen
Of Inner and Outer Chaos—
Insists that I am Goldschmitt.

Coulette, I tell her, Coulette,
Fumbling my money-green passport.
I'm American, gentile,
And there's gas escaping somewhere!
She nods and mutters, Goldschmitt.

There is gas escaping somewhere,
And what does that evil stain
On the mattress signify?

51 Are you sure, are you damned sure,
This isn't the train to Deutschland?

Suddenly, unaccountably,
I sit down and write a letter
To the world, no! to the people
I love, no! to my family, yes!
The Family Goldschmitt.

                                        HENRI COULETTE

The Corridor

A separate place between the thought and felt
The empty hotel corridor was dark.
But here the keyhole shone, a meaning spark.
What fires were latent in it! So he knelt.

Now, at the corridor's much lighter end,
A pierglass hung upon the wall and showed,
As by an easily deciphered code,
Dark, door, and man, hooped by a single band.

He squinted through the keyhole, and within
Surveyed an act of love that frank as air
He was too ugly for, or could not dare,
Or at a crucial moment thought a sin.

Pleasure was simple thus: he mastered it.
If once he acted as participant
He would be mastered, the inhabitant
Of someone else's world, mere shred to fit.

He moved himself to get a better look
And then it was he noticed in the glass

152   Two strange eyes in a fascinated face
That watched him like a picture in a book.

The instant drove simplicity away—
The scene was altered, it depended on
His kneeling, when he rose they were clean gone
The couple in the keyhole; this would stay.

For if the watcher of the watcher shown
There in the distant glass, should be watched too,
Who can be master, free of others; who
Can look around and say he is alone?

Moreover, who can know that what he sees
Is not distorted, that he is not seen
Distorted by a pierglass, curved and lean?
Those curious eyes, through him, were linked to these—

These lovers altered in the cornea's bend.
What could he do but leave the keyhole, rise,
Holding those eyes as equal in his eyes,
And go, one hand held out, to meet a friend?

THOM GUNN

A Camp in the Prussian Forest

I walk beside the prisoners to the road.
Load on puffed load,
Their corpses, stacked like sodden wood,
Lie barred or galled with blood

By the charred warehouse. No one comes today
In the old way

53   To knock the fillings from their teeth;
         The dark, coned, common wreath

         Is plaited for their grave—a kind of grief.
         The living leaf
         Clings to the planted profitable
         Pine if it is able;

         The boughs sigh, mile on green, calm, breathing mile,
         From this dead file
         The planners ruled for them . . . One year
         They sent a million here:

         Here men were drunk like water, burnt like wood.
         The fat of good
         And evil, the breast's star of hope
         Were rendered into soap.

         I paint the star I sawed from yellow pine—
         And plant the sign
         In soil that does not yet refuse
         Its usual Jews

         Their first asylum. But the white, dwarfed star—
         This dead white star—
         Hides nothing, pays for nothing; smoke
         Fouls it, a yellow joke,

         The needles of the wreath are chalked with ash,
         A filmy trash
         Litters the black woods with the death
         Of men; and one last breath

         Curls from the monstrous chimney . . . I laugh aloud
         Again and again;
         The star laughs from its rotting shroud
         Of flesh. O star of men!

                                        RANDALL JARRELL

¹⁵⁴ Drug Store

I do remember an apothecary,
And hereabouts 'a dwells

It baffles the foreigner like an idiom,
And he is right to adopt it as a form

Less serious than the living-room or bar;
        For it disestablishes the cafe,
Is a collective, and on basic country.

Not that it praises hygiene and corrupts
The ice-cream parlor and the tobacconist's
Is it a center; but that the attractive symbols
        Watch over puberty and leer
Like rubber bottles waiting for sick-use.

Youth comes to jingle nickles and crack wise;
The baseball scores are his, the magazines,
Devoted to lust, the jazz, the coca-cola,
        The lending-library of love's latest.
He is the customer; he is heroized.

And every nook and cranny of the flesh
Is spoken to by packages with wiles.
'Buy me, buy me,' they whimper and cajole;
        The hectic range of lipsticks pouts,
Revealing the wicked and the simple mouth.

With scarcely any evasion in their eye
They smoke, undress their girls, exact a stance;
But only for a moment. The clock goes round;
        Crude fellowships are made and lost;
They slump in booths like rags, not even drunk.

KARL SHAPIRO

On the Move

'Man, you gotta Go.'

The blue jay scuffling in the bushes follows
Some hidden purpose, and the gust of birds
That spurts across the field, the wheeling swallows,
Have nested in the trees and undergrowth.
Seeking their instinct, or their poise, or both,
One moves with an uncertain violence
Under the dust thrown by a baffled sense
Or the dull thunder of approximate words.

On motorcycles, up the road, they come:
Small, black, as flies hanging in heat, the Boys,
Until the distance throws them forth, their hum
Bulges to thunder held by calf and thigh.
In goggles, donned impersonality,
In gleaming jackets trophied with the dust,
They strap in doubt—by hiding it, robust—
And almost hear a meaning in their noise.

Exact conclusion of their hardiness
Has no shape yet, but from known whereabouts
They ride, direction where the tires press.
They scare a flight of birds across the field:
Much that is natural, to the will must yield.
Men manufacture both machine and soul,
And use what they imperfectly control
To dare a future from the taken routes.

It is a part solution, after all.
One is not necessarily discord
On earth; or damned because, half animal,
One lacks direct instinct, because one wakes

156 Afloat on movement that divides and breaks.
One joins the movement in a valueless world,
Choosing it, till, both hurler and the hurled,
One moves as well, always toward, toward.

A minute holds them, who have come to go:
The self-defined, astride the created will
They burst away; the towns they travel through
Are home for neither bird nor holiness,
For birds and saints complete their purposes.
At worst, one is in motion; and at best,
Reaching no absolute, in which to rest,
One is always nearer by not keeping still.

THOM GUNN

Black Jackets

In the silence that prolongs the span
Rawly of music when the record ends,
The red-haired boy who drove a van
In weekday overalls but, like his friends,

Wore cycle boots and jacket here
To suit the Sunday hangout he was in,
Heard, as he stretched back from his beer,
Leather creak softly round his neck and chin.

Before him, on a coal-black sleeve
Remote exertion had lined, scratched, and burned
Insignia that could not revive
The heroic fall or climb where they were earned.

On the other drinkers bent together,
Concocting selves for their impervious kit,

He saw it as no more than leather
Which, taut across the shoulders grown to it,

Sent through the dimness of a bar
As sudden and anonymous hints of light
As those that shipping give, that are
Now flickers in the Bay, now lost in night.

He stretched out like a cat, and rolled
The bitterish taste of beer upon his tongue,
And listened to a joke being told:
The present was the things he stayed among.

If it was only loss he wore,
He wore it to assert, with fierce devotion,
Complicity and nothing more.
He recollected his initiation,

And one especially of the rites.
For on his shoulders they had put tattoos:
The group's name on the left, The Knights,
And on the right the slogan Born To Lose.

THOM GUNN

Highway 101, Seal Beach

Young, groomed sullen men of boyless purpose
    Enshrined by coupes
                Shined
                Aligned
Tool around in this wheeled consecration of
                            Unobtainable girls;
And the mileage,
Clocked in the leaded ping of high-octane carburetors

158   Is the low wink of nocturnal celebates
            Premised upon the afterwork solidity
                        Of bored stiffs.
        And they and
                    Other blastoff types
                    At the (traffic) lights
      —In extreme haste to become absolutely nowhere
        Dream of epic nights among the lanes, there
                                    To tear off
        A lot of rubber in the dark,
        Flinging Kleenex & unmentionables
        Along roadless odysseys
        To wave impaled
        As daytime flags
                    For the shrunken science of manhood; then
    Speeding off in all directions
                    None sensed,
                    On low, easy downs,
        They back off and polish;
        Best-selling—as the acne of perfection
                    —another cheek
        To outshine another image of this self.

                                            CURTIS ZAHN

Incident

Once, riding in old Baltimore,
    Heart-filled, head-filled with glee,
I saw a Baltimorean
    Keep looking straight at me.

Now I was eight and very small,
    And he was no whit bigger;

59   And so I smiled, but he poked out
                His tongue, and called me "Nigger."

I saw the whole of Baltimore
        From May until December;
Of all the things that happened there
        That's all that I remember.

COUNTEE CULLEN

Winter Exercise

A man out walking alone in the snow,
Painfully cold, blinded by wind and snow,
And with nowhere in particular to go
But round in a circle, over the wooded hill
And down, back round by the road and past the mill
And up street again to his own doorsill—
Now what may such a man be but a lost
Man, aimlessly battling the snowy host
To get nowhere but home, where his own ghost
Will meet him, bowing, on the parlor floor,
Join him again when he's scarce through the door,
Enjoin him against wandering any more?

Suppose, instead, he really did get lost
There on the hill, beyond surveyor's post
And sidewalk, and Bohemia grew a coast
Which loomed before him, white as the white storm
Blowing into his eyes? With what good form
Would things be kept up by his ghost at the warm
Hearthside at home: His slippers and his drink,
No dust on the floor, or dishes in the sink;
It might be days till anyone would think

160   There was a kind of stillness to all this
Which made the house, though cheerful, an abyss,
And unidentifiably remiss.

Meanwhile his seven-league, left-handed heart
Had kept him circling up there, far apart
From what his ghost, out of domestic art,
Could manage in the way of keeping life
Respectable and decent (keep his wife
From noticing, for instance). His hard strife
Against the storm had long begun to seem
Unduly long, a walk around a dream
Whose nonsense only waking could redeem;
Till, seeing everywhere nothing but deep
Snow and dark woods, he knew he was asleep,
And, to wake up, lay down and went to sleep.

He dreamed a warm, familiar dream of home,
Went, like an auctioneer, from room to room.
Table and chair, razor and brush and comb
He catalogued, and the lady too whose lord
He was, who shared his castle, bed and board,
And realized in his dream that he was bored.
"There's nothing in this for me," he said aloud;
"Better the snow be my lonely shroud."
The ghost at home heard, looked around, allowed
The force of this, and followed: Up the hill
He went, through snow, across the same doorsill
Stepped into dream; and soon the lady will.

HOWARD NEMEROV

Home Town

I go out like a ghost,
nights, to walk the streets

161   I walked fifteen years younger—
seeking my old defeats,
devoured by the old hunger;
I had supposed

this longing and upheaval
had left me with my youth.
Fifteen years gone; once more,
the old lies are the truth:
I must prove I dare,
and the world, and love, is evil.

I have had loves, had such
honors as freely came;
it does not seem to matter.
Boys swagger just the same
along the curbs, or mutter
among themselves and watch.

They're out for the same prize.
And, as the evening grows,
the young girls take the street,
hard, in harlequin clothes,
with black shells on their feet
and challenge in their eyes.

Like a young bitch in her season
she walked the carnival
tonight, trailed by boys;
then, stopped at a penny stall
for me; by glittering toys
the pitchman called the reason

to come and take a chance,
try my hand, my skill.
I could not look; bereft

162   of breath, against my will,
I walked ahead and left
her there without one glance.

Pale soul, consumed by fear
of the living world you haunt,
have you learned what habits lead you
to hunt what you don't want;
learned who does not need you;
learned you are no one here?

W. D. SNODGRASS

Poetry of Departures

Sometimes you hear, fifth-hand,
As epitaph:
He chucked up everything
And just cleared off,
And always the voice will sound
Certain you approve
This audacious, purifying,
Elemental move.

And they are right, I think.
We all hate home
And having to be there:
I detest my room,
Its specially-chosen junk,
The good books, the good bed,
And my life, in perfect order:
So to hear it said

He walked out on the whole crowd
Leaves me flushed and stirred,

53   Like *Then she undid her dress*
Or *Take that you bastard;*
Surely I can, if he did?
And that helps me stay
Sober and industrious.
But I'd go today,

Yes, swagger the nut-strewn roads,
Crouch in the fo'c'sle
Stubbly with goodness, if
It weren't so artificial,
Such a deliberate step backwards
To create an object:
Books; china; a life
Reprehensibly perfect.

PHILIP LARKIN

Going

There is an evening coming in
Across the fields, one never seen before,
That lights no lamps.

Silken it seems at a distance, yet
When it is drawn up over the knees and breast
It brings no comfort.

Where has the tree gone, that locked
Earth to the sky? What is under my hands,
That I cannot feel?

What loads my hands down?

PHILIP LARKIN

164 In Praise of BIC Pens

Others always skip over the word
That will bring the belligerents of the world
To the negotiating table, if only

I can get it written, or will
Teach thin kids in Woetown, West Virginia,
To rebound tough and read Ted Roethke—

I'm writing along in a conspiracy
Of birds and sun and pom-pom girls
Lines to cheer old ladies with shopping bags

Waiting by their busstops at 5 PM
Or lines to get the 12-year-olds off cigarettes
Or save the suicides in gay-bar mensrooms

Or save the fat man from his refrigerator
Or the brilliant boy from color TV
Or the RA private from re-upping for six

Or the whole Midwest from wanting to conquer Asia and
    the Moon
Or the current president from his place in history—
Oh, if only I can get it written

No one will burn kittens or slap little boys or make little girls
    cry
Or cower at cancer or coronaries or plain palsied old age
Or get goofy radiation in his cornflake milk—

If only I can get it written. But always
When I get close to the word and the crowd begins to roar
The common pen skips, leaves the page blank—

But you, BIC pen, at nineteen cents, could trace truce terms
    on tank treads,
Could ratify in the most flourishing script
The amnesty of love for our most dreaded enemies:

The ugly, the poor, the stupid, the sexually screwed-up—
Etching their releases across the slippery communiqués of
    generals and governors,
For Behold you can write upon butter, Yea inscribe even
    through slime!

But at nineteen cents no one pays attention
to the deadwood you shatter or the manifestoes you slice in
    the ice—
For who would believe Truth at *that* price.

                            DAVID HILTON

Good Luck To You Kafka/ You'll Need It Boss

the man from the finance company
came again today he wants to know
when i'm going to pay but what he won't say
is what it was i bought

one morning perhaps when i was high
on poetry and corned jock butties
i must have wandered threepartsmental
into a departmental stare and bought something

a three piece suit for my sweet
a frigidaire to keep frozen my despair
a fitted carpet for the inside of my head

166   he just won't say what it was
and when i laugh he looks the other way
apparently i have only fourteen days left
he won't even say what happens then

i suppose they will come and take away my eyes
(which i know i haven't paid for)
or the words that live inside my head
or my surprise at raindrops or the use

of my legs or my love of bread
then again they just might forget
about me and go away/fat chance

HENRY GRAHAM

The Poet Tries to Turn in His Jock

The way I see it, is that when
I step out on that court and feel
inside that I can't make the plays,
it'll be time to call it quits.

—Elgin Baylor

Going up for the jump shot,
Giving the kid the head-fakes and all
'Til he's jocked right out the door of the gym
And I'm free at the top with the ball and my touch,
Lofting the arc off my fingertips,
I feel my left calf turn to stone
And my ankle warp inward to form when I land
A neat right angle with my leg,
And I'm on the floor,

167   A pile of sweat and sick muscles,
Saying,
Hilton,
You're 29, getting fat,
Can't drive to your right anymore,
You can think of better things to do
On Saturday afternoons than be a chump
For a bunch of sophomore third-stringers;
Join the Y, steam and martinis and muscletone.
But, shit,
The shot goes in.

DAVID HILTON

Supplementary Poems:
For comparison and discussion

I Am

John Clare

The Road Not Taken

Robert Frost

The Unknown Citizen

W. H. Auden

When I Have Fears That I May Cease To Be

John Keats

Ode: Intimations of Immortality from Recollections of Early Childhood

William Wordsworth

Ode: Dejection

Samuel Taylor Coleridge

EDUCA-TION

INTRODUCTION

In a book specifically designed for the contemporary student, it would be a serious omission not to discuss education itself. Modern education in general, and higher education in particular, is undergoing seige from both within and without. Students teachers, administrators, politicians, churchmen, industrialists and groups and committees of every sort have found occasion to be critical of the educational system. Three of the most commonly cited areas of concern are: a tendency toward habitual, almost ritualistic methods and curricula; pragmatic, materialistic-goal orientation; and ever-increasing implicit denials of the worth of the individual. Because of these and other problems, modern education frequently fails to fulfill its basic functions; it fails to introduce the individual to all that makes man unique in the universe and to instill in him an awareness of the ideals that man has developed for the benefit of society.

It is ironic that education, which likes to promote itself as a dynamic, progressive leadership force in society, is usually extremely conservative and resistant to change. Studies of

170 education have indicated that it takes an average of fifteen years to institute significant changes in the educational system, as opposed to five years in medicine or in farming. Small wonder, then, that many of the practices and methods in the profession today are either inappropriate or obsolete.

The continuance of admission policies that are recognized as discriminatory *de facto* as well as *de jure*; the insistence on grading criteria that encourage a belief in grades as ends in themselves rather than means for measuring the effectiveness of the educational process; and dogged resistance to the inclusion in curricula of study areas that have not previously been part of traditional academic pursuits, are but a few examples of the conservatism that continues to permeate modern education.

True, there are many individual educational institutions that are taking the initiative in reorganizing and redirecting their programs, but these are in the minority and they often face great pressure and opposition. Such measures as the inclusion of black studies curricula, the acceptance of the Educational Opportunities Program (EOP), the redistribution of student population in compliance with existing integration laws, to name but a few changes, are more easily implemented than they have been in the past, but in many areas such considerations are still matters of great controversy. And the problem is not entirely quantitative; in some schools the rush to open new programs has clearly shown that there is a need to implement not only new programs, but new programs of quality and lasting value.

Education tends to be habit governed, often to the denial of creativity and innovation. Instead of attempting to fulfill a progressive leadership role, educators habitually seek guidance or, more specifically, expect and accept directives from the community at large. Perhaps they recognize, deep down, the *real* place to which education has been relegated in the hierarchy of society—not leader but servant to the social order. This reality is all too frequently made clear by the community's tendency to be distrustful and disapproving of creative, innovative thought, sometimes to the point of invoking punitive action when such thought cannot be discouraged otherwise. Thus society permits education its illusion of leadership only as long as education, in its goals and actions, is consistent with traditionally accepted norms.

The habit syndrome also manifests itself in other areas, such as the classic organizational structure of schools. Schools have been habitually organized around a traditional authoritative hierarchy with a single non-teaching administrator (answerable only to and contractually dependent upon a Board of Governors representing the community) at the top. Ultimate authority for decision-making has always been in the hands of those at the top, those who are assured of their position by the continuance of the status quo. Such a system can only serve to blunt creativity, not encourage it.

At the classroom level, change or growth is hampered in part by the fact that many educators find themselves directionless in their own profession. No one has ever formulated a consistently successful theory of teaching, a universally aplicable procedural map or itinerary to guide teachers. If society fails to provide them with direction, most individuals use as the basis of their approach to education that which is most convenient to them—the habit patterns they experienced throughout their own education. And so it goes *ad infinitum*— habits continue to govern educational thought and practice.

The need for consistently effective teaching methods is made more acute by demands upon teachers to participate in activities outside the classroom. It is not unusual to find teachers devoting more time to publication, lecture tours and political affairs. Educators at all levels are being offered financially attractive opportunities to participate *directly* in the field in which they have studied and taught for most of their lives.

The academic intellectual is in the forefront of both national and local affairs. Professors of political history are being lured from their ivory towers to run election campaigns or to advise the President on foreign and domestic affairs;

172   journalism professors are acting as press agents for public figures; professors of psychology are directing Madison Avenue and government ad campaigns; professors in various disciplines are operating as consultants for industry. When all this is attempted while the individual continues to teach, he needs time and energy-saving practices in the classroom; instead of researching and teaching new information, he resorts to familiar standby material for class presentation.

Ironically, the educational community often encourages, rather than denies, this condition. A cliché in the profession, most often voiced at the college and university level, is "publish or perish"—get your name in print or get another job. One of the best ways for a scholar to become well known is to publish his work, and the institution with the best-known staff has always been assured the greatest financial support from the government, private organizations, and local citizenry. This economic truth is so fashionable that universities and colleges even go so far as to bestow honorary degrees each year upon people who have never attended any university but who bring with them, in becoming part of the university's "family," personal wealth and prestige. In institutions that subscribe to this philosophy, the preferred teacher is a public figure and therefore a financial asset. The result of such emphasis is that many teachers see their teaching jobs as secondary, necessary only for maintaining them as they pursue other interests and goals, while those who are genuinely interested in teaching often become embittered and disillusioned.

Whether or not he is engaged in selling his services outside the academic community, the conscientious educator is no less aware of the values that hold sway outside. Even the most conscientious, academically emphatic, but student-oriented instructor finds himself influenced. Guided by the desire to do what is best for his students and entrusted with the responsibility of preparing them for the world that awaits them, the dedicated instructor will be tempted to devote his time to teaching what is currently valuable to his students:

173 that is, he will be tempted to teach the very values that have embittered and disillusioned him with his own profession. While these values may not be in the finest tradition of the educational experience, they are what his students will need to compete "out there."

An instructor who fails to provide such emphasis fails to fulfill what society assumes to be a great part of his responsibility. The educational institution, as Dr. Warren Bryan Martin has pointed out, serves modern society "much as the banking and financial institutions [served industrial society] in the earlier stages of industrial development. "These institutions provided not only financing but also much of the executive and managerial talent that guaranteed industry's prosperity. Today, management recruits manpower from the university, and an individual's worth within the managerial class is often determined directly by his academic background. The rewards the student will reap, socially, professionally, and financially, are frequently in direct proportion to how well he learned the pragmatic information, the "truths," so to speak, that govern the profession to which he aspires. For the student whose purpose in attending the university is consistent with such knowledge and training, education is a meaningful experience. For the student who has been nurtured in the belief that the university is something more than a skills-development center, that it embodies the finest ideals of human knowledge and experience, such an education is, at the very least, of questionable value.

Whatever their view of education, all students experience the consequences of another characteristic of modern education—depersonalization. The population explosion of the last two decades, coupled with a realization of the importance of education in modern social division, has resulted in mass education. Schools everywhere are flooded with applications for admission and many of them are finding it impossible to fill the demand. Institutions that were designed to serve a capacity of two to three thousand students are now being required to handle four to five times that many. Where classes once

174 numbered twenty-five or thirty students, two or three hundred now fill the lecture halls. Obviously, such an increase necessitates certain changes, both logistically and instructionally. Logistically, students are processed and programmed by computer: they are assigned a coded sequential number rather than listed alphabetically by name. Instructionally, a teacher cannot personally devote himself to the problems, questions, and doubts of the individual to the same degree that he could with smaller classes. Under these conditions, the instructor becomes little more than a supplier of information. In light of present conditions, it would not be unrealistic to theorize that, as the demand for higher education continues to increase along with the population, any kind of person-to-person instruction will become non-existent. In all probability the computer will find its way into the classroom to perform most, if not all, of the duties of today's instructor. When that happens, the last vestige of personalized education will be a thing of the past.

Even in those institutions where mass education and modern technology have not caused changes in the teacher-student relationship, the student nonetheless is frequently made to feel ignorant and inferior. One might describe the common teacher-student relationship in terms of parent and child. To some degree such a relationship is necessary and beneficial, but education, one might argue, sometimes carries this relationship too far.

Many educators, even at the college level, insist on maintaining the superior-inferior relationship. Faculties and administrations control academic programs, with little or no involvement from the student body. Student government is carefully controlled by the larger government of the institution. Teachers evaluate students constantly, but students are seldom allowed to criticize teachers. If any of these, or similar Establishment-student relationships, are challenged by the student, discipline may be forthcoming. In effect, we continue to maintain a system of education that, in many ways, really operates to the exclusion of the interests of the student—whom it professes to serve.

What are the consequences of an educational system that continues inequities of this kind? There are many, but perhaps the most significant is the feeling of *alienation* that it fosters among students. How can the student be expected to identify with, and respond to, a process that in so many ways denies his validity and his individuality within it; that has adopted, in its programming, administration, and faculties, a life-style contrary to these ideals and purposes it continues to champion; that utilizes methods and materials that have little or no significance to today's student?

An individual who is alienated from a system but forced to participate in it may react in one of two ways—disinterest or open rebellion. In the first instance, the system gives rise to an individual who often seeks to avoid education; in the second instance, it produces a student who attempts to destroy it, either permanently or in order to effect a phoenix-like rebirth of the entire system.

Some student groups and teacher organizations throughout the country have been and currently are in open, frequently violent, rebellion. The Black Student Union, the Third World Liberation Front, Students for a Democratic Society, and the United Federation of Teachers, to name a few, are seeking change through demonstrations of all kinds, ranging from sit-ins to organized strikes at institutions across the nation.

But not all rebellion against contemporary education takes the form of hostile or violent action. Many students are frustrated by certain aspects of the educational process but still want to preserve those qualities that make education an enlightening, inspirational, and pleasurable experience. These people choose other, less punishing methods of dissent. Some of them affirm their validity and deny the depersonalized nature of modern education by taking an active part in educational government, seeking in this manner to promote change in the current status of things; others oppose the current academic life-style by themselves adopting and practicing the life-style of the true academician; still others seek to question methods, materials, and values by speaking out, through all media, whenever the situation demands it.

It is among the non-violent, but nonetheless concerned, involved, and vocal rebels, that we frequently find the contemporary poet. Eloquently, sensitively, gently but forcefully, he speaks out in the best way he knows how whenever he sees education failing to fulfill its promise. It is, of course, *his* voice with which this volume is most concerned.

The Campus on the Hill

Up the reputable walks of old established trees
They stalk, children of the *nouveaux riches*; chimes
Of the tall Clock Tower drench their heads in blessing:
"I don't wanna play at your house;
"I don't like you any more."
My house stands opposite, on the other hill,
Among meadows, with the orchard fences down and falling;
Deer come almost to the door.
You cannot see it, even in this clearest morning.
White birds hang in the air between
Over the garbage landfill and those homes thereto adjacent,
Hovering slowly, turning, settling down
Like the flakes sifting imperceptibly onto the little town
In a waterball of glass.
And yet, this morning, beyond this quiet scene,
The floating birds, the backyards of the poor,
Beyond the shopping plaza, the dead canal, the hillside
    lying tilted in the air,
Tomorrow has broken out today:
Riot in Algeria, in Cyprus, in Alabama;

177 Aged in wrong, the empires are declining,
And China gathers, soundlessly, like evidence.
What shall I say to the young on such a morning?—
Mind is the one salvation?—also grammar?—
No; my little ones lean not toward revolt. They
Are the Whites, the vaguely furiously driven, who resist
Their souls with such passivity
As would make Quakers swear. All day, dear Lord, all day
They wear their godhead lightly.
They look out from their hill and say,
To themselves, "We have nowhere to go but down;
The great destination is to stay."
Surely the nations will be reasonable;
They look at the world—don't they?—the world's way?
The clock just now has nothing more to say.

W. D. SNODGRASS

Spring Revue

The folk group chopped its last note clean
and bowed. The lights went up on hands
caught in mid-clap.

            I settled back;
they ran things right at this school.
What good's a Spring Revue, with no
spring in its step?

Not like at our son's school, where
humor black with char passes for fun
and lays, heavy and undigested,
on the mind.

            This crowd, too
more up-lift, its crowd-coo gay,

clothes tidy as a pin. Not calling
for apologies to kin.

Two coeds near me
chattered, and I listened in. With
hair like shiny helmets, faces bright,
they probed another spring-time
happening—the batch of kitties—what
can be done?

The eager words poured
out, "So we just flushed them down the
toilet, one by one," and girlish heads
exchanged contented nods.

The light dimmed warning
and the crowd poured back, and I was gripped
by longing fierce as grief, for bearded,
long-haired youth that hold no brief for
cleanliness or God, but press themselves
in straggly picket lines because they
care, that little people die, somewhere.

CHARLOTTE MORTIMER

The Student

"In America," began
the lecturer, "everyone must have a
degree. The French do not think that
all can have it, they don't say everyone
    must go to college." We
do incline to feel
    that although it may be unnecessary

79   to know fifteen languages,
one degree is not too much. With us, a
school—like the singing tree of which
the leaves were mouths singing in concert—is
     both a tree of knowledge
and of liberty,—
     seen in the unanimity of college

mottoes, *lux et veritas,*
Christo et ecclesiae, sapiet
felici. It may be that we
have not knowledge, just opinions, that we
     are undergraduates,
not students; we know
     we have been told with smiles, by expatriates

of whom we had asked "When will
your experiment be finished?" "Science
is never finished." Secluded
from domestic strife, Jack Bookworm led a
     college life, says Goldsmith;
and here also as
     in France or Oxford, study is beset with

dangers,—with bookworms, mildews,
and complaisancies. But someone in New
England has known enough to say
the student is patience personified,
     is a variety
of hero, "patient
     of neglect and of reproach,"—who can "hold by

himself." You can't beat hens to
make them lay. Wolf's wool is the best of wool,
but it cannot be sheared because
the wolf will not comply. With knowledge as

180   with the wolf's surliness,
the student studies
     voluntarily, refusing to be less

than individual. He
"gives his opinion and then rests on it;"
he renders service when there is
no reward, and is too reclusive for
     some things to seem to touch
him, not because he
     has no feeling but because he has so much.

MARIANNE MOORE

In America*

In the following annotations, Marianne Moore suggests how phrases from her reading and observation are fitted, in the manner of mosaics, into the text of her poem:

"In America." Les Idéals de l'Education Française; lecture, December 3, 1931, by M. Auguste Desclos, Director-adjoint, Office National des Universités et Ecoles Françaises de Paris.

The singing tree. Each leaf was a mouth, and every leaf joined in concert. *Arabian Nights.*

Lux et veritus (Yale); *Christo et ecclesiae* (Harvard); sapiet felici,—

* [These annotations for "The Student" demonstrate how Marianne Moore has used phrases from her reading and observation in writing this poem—Ed. note.]

"Science is never finished." Professor Einstein
to an American student; *New York Times*.

Jack Bookworm in Goldsmith's
The Double Transformation.

A variety of hero: Emerson in *The American Scholar*;
"there can be no scholar without the heroic
mind;" "let him hold by himself; . . .
patient of neglect, patient of reproach."

The wolf. Edmund Burke, November, 1781, in
reply to Fox: "there is excellent wool on the
back of a wolf and therefore he must be
sheared. . . . But will he comply?"

"Gives his opinion." Henry McBride in the *New York
Sun*, December 12, 1931: "Dr. Valentiner . . . has
the typical reserve of the student. He does not enjoy
the active battle of opinion that invariably rages
when a decision is announced that can be
weighed in great sums of money. He gives
his opinion firmly and rests upon that."

MARIANNE MOORE

The Student

Under the rusting elms his separate path,
Crossing and recrossing the separate paths
Of others like himself, whose aimless feet
Weave some invisible pattern on the grass,
Takes him to the classroom, to his seat,
Where he walks on words toward a drowning man
He dimly imagines, or pictures in vague dreams,

182   A shifty man whose face he thinks familiar
As his own, yet cannot fix exactly,
Who calls to him when he walks out again
Onto the solid earth to thread his way
Under the rusting elm leaves, which float down
Like nets through water seeking the vagrant school.

DABNEY STUART

The Three Movements

It is not in the books
that he is looking, nor for
a new book, nor
documents of any kind, nor
does he expect it to be like the wind,
that, when you touch it, tears
without a sound of tearing, nor
like the rain
water
that becomes
grass in the sun. He
expects that when he finds it,
it will be
like a man, visible, alive
to what has happened and what
will happen, with
firmness in its face, seeing
exactly what is, without
measure of change, and not
like documents,
or rain in the grass.

But what, he says,
if it is not
for the finding, not

83 what you most expect, nor even
what you dread, nothing
but the books, the endless
documents, the banked
volumes that repeat
mile after mile
their names,
their information?
Perhaps there is nothing
except the rain
water
becoming the grass, the
sustenance. What
a man should do is
accumulate
information
until he has gathered, like a
farmer, as much
as his resources can contain.

Yet perhaps, he thinks,
I speak
with knowledge, but perhaps
forgetting the movement
that intrigues
all thinking. It is
the movement which works through,
which discovers itself
in alleys, in
sleep, not
expected and not
in the books of words and phrases
nor the various paints and edges
of scenery.
It is, he says,
familiar when come upon,
glimpsed

184   as in a mirror
unpredicted,
and it appears
to understand. It is
like himself, only visible.

DONALD HALL

Empty Holds a Question

I saw him brought into Emergency,
reduced, behind his life-pressed scowl, to fear.
He'd been my teacher of geometry—
a tall, proud man behind a quizzing frown,
who'd pulled the theorems off the printed page
and called Infinity to being in my mind.
He'd said, "All things can be, quite logically,
defined with mathematics."
I was the one white uniform that wore a face—
he trusted me and signed the space that he'd refused before.
Presurgery, I took his pulse, all platitudes and hope . . .
But he did not return . . .
And so,
could not trace out for me
how I could be at twenty-two
as old as all mankind.

PAT FOLK

To David, about His Education

The world is full of mostly invisible things,
And there is no way but putting the mind's eye,
Or its nose, in a book, to find them out,
Things like the square root of Everest

85   Or how many times Byron goes into Texas,
Or whether the law of the excluded middle
Applies west of the Rockies. For these
And the like reasons, you have to go to school
And study books and listen to what you are told,
And sometimes try to remember. Though I don't know
What you will do with the mean annual rainfall
On Plato's Republic, or the calorie content
Of the Diet of Worms, such things are said to be
Good for you, and you will have to learn them
In order to become one of the grown-ups
Who sees invisible things neither steadily nor whole,
But keeps gravely the grand confusion of the world
Under his hat, which is where it belongs,
And teaches small children to do this in their turn.

HOWARD NEMEROV

Classes

they should be held in the open.
free. you should talk, then I:
we will have communion, here under
the bright green leaves of a Spring
all will remember as our awakening.

class, I'm talking to you.
it's important we touch each other,
no matter how foolish the gesture
(this connection, couldn't matter less—
who but a fool cares about commas?

         I am here,
you, there. ah, but you sleep.
& I drowse. at least we share
this room, let that be recorded:

186   together, we dream these hours
and, perhaps, each other.

class. I hear your names
like strokes against ancient cymbals,
ghosts, voices answering to a role.
class. we are dying, do you know
that? mustn't we speak, now? or
for God's sake let's end this farce,
let tree roots claim us, spreading
its branches to the sky, let us live
that way, if we can manage no other.

KEITH WILSON

Education

Now to the dry hillside,
Terraced with crumbling limestone,
Where there were vineyards long ago,
Evening comes cool and violet
Under the olive trees, and only
The almond blossoms and the first stars
Are alight. Your fine lean hand
Like a spindle of light
Moves as you talk, as if
You were conducting a slow music.
What are you talking about?
You are explaining everything to me—
The abandoned olive grove,
The walls older than the Romans,
The flowering almond tree,
And the twilight darkening
Around the stars and around
Your speaking lips and moving hand.

KENNETH REXROTH

Absent-Minded Professor

This lonely figure of not much fun
Strayed out of folklore fifteen years ago
Forever. Now on an autumn afternoon,
While the leaves drift past the office window,
His bright replacement, present-minded, stays
At the desk correcting papers, nor ever grieves
For the silly scholar of the bad old days,
Who'd burn the paper and correct the leaves.

HOWARD NEMEROV

University Examinations in Egypt

The air is thick with nerves and smoke: pens tremble in
        sweating hands:
Domestic police flit in and out, with smelling salts and aspirin:
And servants, grave-faced but dirty, pace the aisles,
With coffee, Players and Coca-Cola.

Was it like this in my day, at my place? Memory boggles
Between the aggressive fly and curious ant—but did I really?
Pause in my painful flight to light a cigarette or swallow
        drugs?

The nervous eye, patrolling these hot unhappy victims,
Flinches at the symptoms of a year's hard teaching—
'Falstaff indulged in drinking and sexcess', and then,
'Doolittle was a dusty man' and 'Dr. Jonson edited the
        Yellow Book.'

Culture and aspirin: the urgent diploma, the straining brain—
        all in the evening fall
To tric-trac in the café, to Hollywood in the picture-house:

188   Behind, like tourist posters, the glamour of laws and
        committees,
    Wars for freedom, cheap textbooks, national aspirations—

    And, farther, still and very faint, the foreign ghost of happy
        Shakespeare,
    Keats who really loved things, Akhenaton who adored the
        Sun,
    And Goethe who never thought of Thought.

D. J. ENRIGHT

April Inventory

The green catalpa tree has turned
All white; the cherry blooms once more.
In one whole year I haven't learned
A blessed thing they pay you for.
The blossoms snow down in my hair;
The trees and I will soon be bare.

The trees have more than I to spare.
The sleek, expensive girls I teach,
Younger and pinker every year,
Bloom gradually out of reach.
The pear tree lets its petals drop
Like dandruff on a tabletop.

The girls have grown so young by now
I have to nudge myself to stare.
This year they smile and mind me how
My teeth are falling with my hair.
In thirty years I may not get
Younger, shrewder, or out of debt.

39   The tenth time, just a year ago,
I made myself a little list
Of all the things I'd ought to know,
Then told my parents, analyst,
And everyone who's trusted me
I'd be substantial, presently.

I haven't read one book about
A book or memorized one plot.
Or found a mind I did not doubt.
I learned one date. And then forgot.
And one by one the solid scholars
Get the degrees, the jobs, the dollars.

And smile above their starchy collars.
I taught my classes Whitehead's notions;
One lovely girl, a song of Mahler's.
Lacking a source-book or promotions,
I showed one child the colors of
A luna moth and how to love.

I taught myself to name my name,
To bark back, loosen love and crying;
To ease my woman so she came,
To ease an old man who was dying.
I have not learned how often I
Can win, can love, but choose to die.

I have not learned there is a lie
Love shall be blonder, slimmer, younger;
That my equivocating eye
Loves only by my body's hunger;
That I have forces, true to feel,
Or that the lovely word is real.

While scholars speak authority
And wear their ulcers on their sleeves,

190   My eyes in spectacles shall see
These trees procure and spend their leaves.
There is a value underneath
The gold and silver in my teeth.

Though trees turn bare and girls turn wives,
We shall afford our costly seasons;
There is a gentleness survives
That will outspeak and has its reasons.
There is a loveliness exists,
Preserves us, not for specialists.

W. D. SNODGRASS

On Flunking A Nice Boy
Out of School

I wish I could teach you how ugly
decency and humility can be when they are not
the election of a contained mind but only
the defenses of an incompetent. Were you taught
meekness as a weapon? Or did you discover,
by chance maybe, that it worked on mother
and was generally a good thing—
at least when all else failed—to get you over
the worst of what was coming? Is that why you bring
these sheep-faces to Tuesday?
                    They won't do.
It's three months' work I want, and I'd sooner have it
from the brassiest lumpkin in pimpledom, but have it
than all these martyred repentances from you.

JOHN CIARDI

191 Kindergarten Teacher

Her intentions are to see that Blue
Is never painted next to Green,
And that the sexes use separate toilets.
Governed by the laws of washbasins, the
Children become little domestics
Of her hysteria.

Her spirit is like a wilderness;
Her face has no water hole. Every
Sham can burp her, any psychopath can
Have her for dessert. If she does love
Something she makes a meal out of it.
A few gray hairs
Are the extent of her ideas.

Today, while the boys and girls
Rest upon their backs, she plans
Her summer trip. Tickets
Take her nowhere.

She belongs to that all-powerful,
International body: The Association
For the Advancement of the Idea
That Intractable Children
Be Given Off As Vapor.

STANLEY KIESEL

On Returning to Teach

At a distance, young voices are whooping,
to which my stately, fostering mother

192   pays no heed. But as the moon bears
with great heaviness waters to itself,
one tongue reissues for attention.
It is mine. I have come back to win
the National Book Award, but am locked in
the English Department, let me out!

My friends rally round. They were expected to
do this. With refrains. Tunes. Lips.
With brace and bit and biting epigram
they bore the walls, release and welcome me.
At once I wish to share in their spirits,
their fitting wits and sensual nostalgia.
The short lines in my palms seem to lengthen,
and the slapping of their thighs sounds tender.

I have been rescued before my black angels
and merely observed their disappearance, have walked
in the corroidor when the one door opened—
and entered, and asked for the moon, and laughed;
have wanted for a hand, a back and a brain,
and have wanted my women to tell me again.
In the second childhood, there are not more children.
In the second semester, the teachers are older.

MARVIN BELL

University

To hurt the Negro and avoid the Jew
Is the curriculum. In mid-September
The entering boys, identified by hats,
Wander in a maze of mannered brick
    Where boxwood and magnolia brood

193   And columns with imperious stance
Like rows of ante-bellum girls
     Eye them, outlanders.

In whited cells, on lawns equipped for peace,
Under the arch, and lofty banister,
Equals shake hands, unequals blankly pass;
The exemplary weather whispers "Quiet, quiet"
     And visitors on tiptoe leave
     For the raw North, the unfinished West,
     As the young, detecting an advantage,
          Practice a face.

Where, on their separate hill, the colleges,
Like manor house of an older law,
Gaze down embankments on a land in fee,
The Deans, dry spinsters over family plate,
     Ring out the English name like coin,
     Humor the slob and lure the lout.
     Within the precincts of this world
          Poise is a club.

But on the neighboring range, misty and high,
The past is absolute: some luckless race
Dull with inbreeding and conformity
Wears out its heart, and comes barefoot and bad
     For charity or jail. The scholar
     Sanctions their obsolete disease;
     The gentleman revolts with shame
          At his ancestor.

And the true nobleman, once a democrat,
Sleeps on his private mountain. He was one
Whose thought was shapely and whose dream was broad;
This school he held his heart and epitaph.
     But now it takes from him his name,

194   Falls open like a dishonest look,
And shows us, rotten and endowed,
Its senile pleasure.

KARL SHAPIRO

Supplementary Poems:
For comparison and discussion

When I Heard The Learn'd Astronomer
Walt Whitman

Musophilus
Alexander Pope

The Scholar Gypsy
Matthew Arnold

Rugby Chapel
Matthew Arnold

A Grammarian's Funeral
Robert Browning

The Prelude—Books 1 & 5
William Wordsworth

Letter to Lord Byron
W. H. Auden

An Elementary School Classroom in a Slum
Stephen Spender

The Mind Is An Enchanting Thing
Marianne Moore

Essay On Criticism
Samuel Daniel

THE CITY

INTRODUCTION

As recently as 1920, America could have been described as an agrarian nation; the rich farmlands and many small towns and cities scattered across the continent attracted a majority of its 100 million citizens. Although little more than 50 years have elapsed since that time, the nation has undergone a profound change.

America still has many rich farmlands and small towns that stretch from coast to coast, but now more than 80 percent of its 190 million population lives huddled together in urban centers. Farm life, small town life, has been exchanged for urban dwelling by most Americans.

At first people moved from farms and small towns into the city, but the city became packed with people, garbage, smog, and buildings. When concrete replaced grass and trees, many people moved out of the city, looking for clean air, green life, and room to stretch. But they did not go back to the farms; the cities still held them close. Suburbs grew up near the cities, suburbs filled with people who wanted the best of both worlds. As suburb merged with suburb, reaching farther in all directions, great urban areas began to surround and choke the cities. The two giant population masses of today were created, centering around America's two largest cities—New York,

196 with its megalopolis that extends from Boston to Washington, and Los Angeles, with its megalopolis that extends from Santa Barbara to the Mexican border.

How has the change in distribution affected man and his poetry? How does life in the core city affect man's relationship to his fellow man when he no longer knows his neighbors? He is surrounded by an ever-changing mass of people, physically much closer—just behind the paper-thin apartment wall—but in many ways far more distant than the neighbor a quarter of a mile down the road back in Kansas.

How are man's values affected when he is faced with life in a ghetto, surrounded by hate, violence, and disregard for property on every hand? Often ghetto apartments are not locked because the doors would be smashed by thieves or vandals; children in today's slums die of rat bite; garbage is piled carelessly in every alley. How does life in the core city affect man's notion of beauty when he sees ugly, dilapidated, unrepaired, and unkempt dwellings crowded to bursting with too many families and too many children. Blue skies, clouds and rainbows are obscured by the gray-black, eye-burning, chest-aching air pollution.

The poetry of the core city reflects man's response to his environment: his depersonalization, his despair, his anger generated by this life. Earlier poets, such as Sandburg, Whitman, MacLeish, and Blake, tell of the hustle, excitement, power, and growth of the city. Contemporary poets describe the decay.

What then of suburbia? Far more people live in the suburbs than in the core city. The San Fernando Valley, an aggregate of suburbs northwest of Los Angeles, contains more people than Pittsburgh, Pennsylvania. What of the millions of urban dwellers who sleep outside the core city? What does commuting mean to these men when the ride on trains and freeways takes up nearly half of their waking leisure hours. What is the effect of snarled traffic, endless waiting, noise, and confusion? What of wives and families waiting at home for the commuting husbands to finish their ten or twelve hour

197 days? Boredom and distance creep in; children see less of their fathers; wives go their own way to clubs, work, or the television set. What effect does this life have on suburban man's relationship to his family?

The move from the city, meant as an escape from crowds and ugliness, still finds the suburban man surrounded by smog, freeway ramps, shopping centers and neighbors too near for a comfortably loud party or quarrel. How does life in a housing development affect man's notion of beauty when he is faced with row upon row of air-conditioned houses, each identical to his, each with an indentical, handkerchief-sized lawn? How does life in a suburb of sameness affect man's values and his sense of unique worth when his neighbors wear the same style clothes, buy the same kind of new car, mow their same small square of green with an identical power mower at the same time Sunday morning? The poetry of suburbia reflects man's response to this life: his boredom, his isolation, his loss of self identity.

In the city, man moves away from the masses that are always too close; he withdraws into himself. He protects himself from the encroachment of others by walling off part of his response to them, by becoming indifferent to their lives, their needs, and even their cries for help. Contemporary poets reflect this withdrawal and estrangement.

City man sees machines, cement, and broken buildings; he hears horns, sirens, and the clash of metal; he smells fumes and smoke. Contemporary poets express the concerns of the city by using symbols drawn from their own urban experiences. Life in the city is quick, staccato, tense, restless, striving. Contemporary poets of the city reflect this pace in the rhythm of their poetry; they do not try to express the leisure and peace that the city dweller has never felt.

Look now at the poems of the city—the core city and the suburbs. How do the poets convey a sense of the lives of the people who live there? How do these poets show their special view of the world, their dreams, their hopes, and their despair?

198 Grief

I

A fireman enters. He entertains us
With his water-gun, struts around the building,
Warns us not to "use the incinerator."
"What shall we use?"
The fireman enters the flame,
The buildings burns. He waves inside the ruins.

II

I placed inside my hair,
After the flames,
Three peacock feathers, each
With a perfect quill.
I know they will change with the color of morning light
As eyes take on new colors when we cry.
I placed inside my hair
A new eyesight. The peacock walks my forehead as I lie
Alone.

III

Grief enters new cities on
A match-stick.
Grief's in the garage, Grief's in
The windshield; Grief
Is the fireman.

SANDRA HOCHMAN

Cold Water Flat

Come to conquer
this living Labyrinth of rock,
young Theseus of Dubuque
finds he is mazed without a minotaur,
without his Ariadne in the dark.

He dreams beyond
his steelwalled fear to fields grown
vertical with corn
and hope. Home to this heroic end:
imprisoned in the city of alone;

here smog obscures
his visionary victor's world
and streetsounds dulled
with rain reverberate in airshaft hours
where braver conquerors have been felled.

Amazed at night,
stalking the seven maids no sword
can save, he is devoured
in passageways of reinforced concrete,
trapped by his beast, and overpowered

in sleepless dead-
end dreams. How now, Theseus? How send
word home you are confined
with neither wings nor lover's thread
in the city that a murderer designed?

PHILIP BOOTH

200   Morning Song

Look, it's morning, and a little water gurgles in the tap.
I wake up waiting, because it's Sunday, and turn twice more
than usual in bed, before I rise to cereal and comic strips.
I have risen to the morning danger and feel proud,
and after shaving off the night's disguises, after searching
close to the bone for blood, and finding only a little,
I shall walk out bravely into the daily accident.

ALAN DUGAN

What Happened?
What Do You Expect?

The waiter waited, the cook ate,
the scales read zero, and the clock
began to agree. It agreed
and disagreed but rang no bells,
and in the quiet of the whole
peeled onion on the chopping block
the whole flayed lamb stamped
     QUALITY
hung by its heels and was
devoured by a fly. Outside,
a woman screamed and stopped.
Two cops came in for coffee-and,
laughing and filling the place
with night as black as the sweat
in the armpits of their shirts.
"Some guy hit his girl friend
and she didn't like it or us
either." Oh it had been
the count-down for a great

catastrophe that had not
happened, not as raw event,
but as time in the death of the lamb.

ALAN DUGAN

On Hurricane Jackson

Now his nose's bridge is broken, one eye
will not focus and the other is a stray;
trainers whisper in his mouth while one ear
listens to itself, clenched like a fist;
generally shadow-boxing in a smoky room,
his mind hides like the aching boys
who lost a contest in the Pan-Hellenic games
and had to take the back roads home,
but someone else, his perfect youth,
laureled in newsprint and dollar bills,
triumphs forever on the great white way
to the statistical Sparta of the champs.

ALAN DUGAN

The Bay Bridge
From Portrero Hill

Pure
Every day there's the bridge
Every day there's the bridge
Every day there's the bridge
Every day there's the bridge
And each night.
It's not easy to live this way.

202   Once
The bridge was small and stone-white
And called the Pont au Change
Or the Point Louis Phillippe.
We went home at midnight
To the Ile Saint Louis as deer
Through a rustle of bells.
Six years distant
And the Atlantic
And a continent.
The way I was then
And the way I am now.
A long time.

I fed in the bright parts of the forest,
Stinting to pass among the impali.
But one can acquire a taste for love
As for loneliness
Or ugliness
As for saintliness.
Each a special way of going down.

That was a sweet country
And large.
Ample with esplanades,
Easy with apricots.
A happy country.
But a country for children.

Now
Every day there's the bridge.
Every day there's the exacting,
Literal, foreign country of the heart.
Toads and panders
Ruined horses
Pears

3   Terrifying honey
Heralds
Heralds

JACK GILBERT

The Dial Tone

A moment of silence, first, then there it is.
But not as though it only now began
Because of my attention; rather, this,
That I begin at one point on its span
Brief kinship with its endless going on.

Between society and self it poses
Neutrality perceptible to sense,
Being a no man's land the lawyer uses
Much as the lover does: charged innocence,
It sits on its own electrified fence,

Is neither pleased nor hurt by race results
Or by the nasty thing John said to Jane;
Is merely interrupted by insults,
Devotions, lecheries; after the sane
And mad hang up at once, it will remain.

Suppose that in God a black bumblebee
Or colorless hummingbird buzzed at night,
Dividing the abyss up equally;
And carried its neither sweetness nor its light
Across impossible eternity.

Now take this hummingbird, this bee, away;
And like the Cheshire smile without its cat
The remnant hum continues on its way,

204   Unwinged, able at once to move and wait,
An endless freight train on an endless flat.

Something like that, some loneliest of powers
That never has confessed its secret name.
I do not doubt that if you gave it hours
And then last patience, it would be the same
After you left that it was before you came.

HOWARD NEMEROV

Thesis, Antithesis, and Nostalgia

Not even dried-up leaves,
skidding like ice-boats on
their points down winter streets,
can scratch the surface of
a child's summer and its wealth:
a stagnant calm that seemed
as if it must go on and on
outside of cyclical variety
the way, at child-height on a wall,
a brick named "Ann"
by someone's piece of chalk
still loves the one named "Al"
although the street is vacant and
the writer and the named are gone.

ALAN DUGAN

Malvolio in San Francisco

Two days ago they were playing the piano
With a hammer and blowtorch.
Next week they will read poetry
To saxophones.

5   And always they are building the Chinese Wall
    Of laughter.
    They laugh so much.
    So much more than I do.
    And it doesn't wear them out
    As it wears me out.
    That's why your poetry's no good,
    They say.
    You should turn yourself upside down
    So your ass would stick out,
    They say.
    And they seem to know.

    They are right, of course.
    I do feel awkward playing the game.
    I do play the clown badly.
    I cannot touch easily.
    But I mistrust the ways of this city
    With its white skies and weak trees.
    One finds no impali here.
    And the birds are pigeons.
    The first rate seems unknown
    In this city of easy fame.
    The hand's skill is always
    From deliberate labor.

    They put Phidias in prison
    About his work on the Parthenon,
    Saying he had stolen gold.
    And he probably had.
    Those who didn't try to body Athena
    They stayed free.

    And Orpheus probably invited the rending
    By his stubbon alien smell.
    Poor Orpheus.
    Who lost so much by making the difficult journey
    When he might have grieved

206   Easily.
Who tried to go back among the living
With the smell of journey on him.
Poor Orpheus
His stubborn tongue
Blindly singing all the way to Lesbos.

What if I should go yellow-stockinged
And cross-gartered?
Suppose I did smile
Fantastically,
Kissed my hand to novelty,
What then?
Still would they imprison me in their dark house.
They would taunt me as doctors
Concerned for my health
And laugh.
Always that consuming,
Unrelenting laughter.

The musk deer is beguiled down from the great mountain
By flutes
To be fastened in a box
And tortured for the smell of his pain.

Yet somehow
There is somehow

I long for my old bigotry.

JACK GILBERT

Constructions: Upper East Side

Wreckers
Drilling and breaking rock
As if New York were one great tooth

207　Rotten but smiling.
Gloria sits in her studio drilling and breaking boxes.
She is not setting foundations; she is making horses
Talk. She is dis-embalming dolls.
In Manhattan everything is being torn from rock,
Our buildings break. Even the ball,
The gong-ball destroying our buildings,
Breaks. Even tools
Built for destruction break.

Outside my window wreckers
Trapped in constructions: blond
And black men under helmets of steel, caught in earth. . .
Killing earth. The earth is taken somewhere else.
Where does all the earth go?
Wreckers in uniforms of mesh ride
Jackhammers and dust-machines, gripping
Torches of fire. They are precise. Sea shells,
The French horn, animal and vegetable are streamlined.

Drills,
The drills sound in my head. I toss words
Back at them. I throw them down as part
Of a new foundation.
I hang words over glass.

Who will escape
This tyranny of the T square?
Gloria, commissioned by
No-one, sets up her broken dolls.

Riding past mirrors and new office buildings,
She tries to construct
A small tower out of ivory and horn.
Dreams are nails. Her daydreams ring
On linoleum. Here, the man
Who dropped the bomb on Hiroshima, and went insane,
Grabs back his bomb again.

She's shrinking the jowl and the paunch of Diamond Jim Brady
To clean lines.
Glass is broken.

SANDRA HOCHMAN

A Picture

Of people running down the street
Among the cars, a good many people.
You could see that something was up,
Because people in American towns
Don't ordinarily run, they walk,
And not in the street. The camera caught
A pretty girl tilted off-balance
And with her mouth in O amazed;
A man in a fat white shirt, his tie
Streaming behind him, as one flat foot
Went slap on the asphalt—you could see
He was out of breath, but dutifully
Running along with all the others,
Maybe at midday, on Main Street somewhere.

The running faces did not record
Hatred or anger or great enthusiasm
For what they were doing (hunting down
A Negro, according to the caption),
But seemed rather solemn, intent,
With the serious patience of animals
Driven through a gate by some
Urgency out of the camera's range,
On an occasion too serious
For private feeling. The breathless faces
Expressed a religion of running,
A form of ritual exaltation

209 Devoted to obedience, and
Obedient, it might be, to the Negro,
Who was not caught by the camera
When it took the people in the street
Among the cars, toward some object,
Seriously running.

HOWARD NEMEROV

Ditty

The very dead of night: no noise
Mounts from the avenue; no smoke
Uncoils to an unspotted snake
Rubbing black skin against the skies.

What act of violence prepares
Emergence from a midnight dream?
What murder murders murder's name
In a mute room of settled fears?

Fugitive silence! . . . Now here, now there,
The traffic of the world begins
Restoring men to daily sins
That are fulfilled with practiced care.

In dark, in day, self is the self,
Does what it does and then affirms
The several slaughters it performs,
Calling necessity the wolf.

No pestilence, no civil blight,
Alters the habit fixed to breath:
Men feed on blood, we want more death,
And live in love of appetite.

ROGER HECHT

210 Working on Wall Street

What's left of the sunset's watered blood
settles between the slabs of Wall Street.
Winter rubs the sky bruise-blue as flesh.
We head down into the subway, glad
the cars are padded with bodies so we
keep warm. Emptied from tall closets
where we work, on the days' shelves
reached by elevators, the heap of us,   .
pressed by iron sides, dives forward under
the city—parcels shipped out in a trunk.

The train climbs its cut to the trestle.
Sunset's gone. Those slabs across the murky
river have shrunk to figurines, reflecting
the blush of neon—a dainty tableau, all
pink, on the dresser-top of Manhattan—
eclipsed as we sink into the tunnel.
The train drops and flattens for the long
bore under Brooklyn.

Night, a hiatus hardly real, tomorrow
this double rut of steel will racket us back
to the city. We, packages in the trade
made day after day, will tumble out of
hatches on The Street, to be met by swags
of wind that scupper off those roofs
(their upper windows blood-filled by the sun.)
Delivered into lobbies, clapped into upgoing
cages, sorted to our compartments, we'll be
stamped once more for our wages.

MAY SWENSON

Learning By Doing

"constructive technological destructiveness"
—Marcuse, Eros & Civilization

They're taking down a tree at the front door,
The power saw is snarling at some nerves,
Whining at others. Now and then it grunts,
And sawdust falls like snow or a drift of seeds.

Rotten, they tell us, at the fork, and one
Big wind would bring it down. So what do they do
They do, as usual, to do us good.
Whatever cannot carry its own weight
Has got to go, and so on; you expect
To hear them talking next about survival
And the values of a free society.
For in the explanations people give
On these occasions there is generally some
Mean-spirited moral point, and everyone
Privately wonders if his neighbors plan
To saw him up before he falls on them.

Maybe a hundred years in sun and shower
Dismantled in a morning and let down
Out of itself a finger at a time
And then an arm, and so down to the trunk,
Until there's nothing left to hold on to
Or snub the splintery holding rope around,
And where those big green divagations were
So loftily with shadows interleaved
The absent-minded blue rains in on us.

212   Now that they've got it sectioned on the ground
It looks as though somebody made a plain
Error in diagnosis, for the wood
Is sweet and sound throughout. You couldn't know,
Of course, until you took it down. That's what
Experts are for, and these experts stand round
The giant pieces of tree as though expecting
An instruction booklet from the factory
Before they try to put it back together.

Anyhow, there it isn't on the ground.
Next come the tractor and the crowbar crew
To extirpate what's left and fill the grave.
Maybe tomorrow grass seed will be sown.
There's some mean-spirited moral point in that
As well: you learn to bury your mistakes,
Though for a while at dusk the darkening air
will be with many shadows interleaved,
And pierced with a bewilderment of birds.

HOWARD NEMEROV

An Urban Convalescence

Out for a walk, after a week in bed,
I find them tearing up part of my block
And, chilled through, dazed and lonely, join the dozen
In meek attitudes, watching a huge crane
Fumble luxuriously in the filth of years.
Her jaws dribble rubble. An old man
Laughs and curses in her brain,
Bringing to mind the close of *The White Goddess*.

As usual in New York, everything is torn down
Before you have had time to care for it.
Head bowed, at the shrine of noise, let me try to recall

213   What building stood here. Was there a building at all?
I have lived on this same street for a decade.

Wait. Yes. Vaguely a presence rises
Some five floors high, of shabby stone
—Or am I confusing it with another one
In another part of town, or of the world?—
And over its lintel into focus vaguely
Misted with blood (my eyes are shut)
A single garland sways, stone fruit, stone leaves,
Which years of grit had etched until it thrust
Roots down, even into the poor soil of my seeing.
When did the garland become part of me?
I ask myself, amused almost,
Then shiver once from head to toe,

Transfixed by a particular cheap engraving of garlands
Bought for a few francs long ago,
All calligraphic tendril and cross-hatched rondure,
Ten years ago, and crumpled up to stanch
Boughs dripping, whose white gestures filled a cab,
And thought of neither then nor since.
Also, to clasp them, the small, red-nailed hand
Of no one I can place. Wait. No. Her name, her features
Lie toppled underneath that year's fashions.
The words she must have spoken, setting her face
To fluttering like a veil, I cannot hear now,
Let alone understand.

So that I am already on the stair,
As it were, of where I lived,
When the whole structure shudders at my tread
And soundlessly collapses, filling
The air with motes of stone.
Onto the still erect building next door
Are pressed levels and hues—

214   Pocked rose, streaked greens, brown whites.
Who drained the pousse-café?
Wires and pipes, snapped off at the roots, quiver.

Well, that is what life does. Stare
A moment longer, so. And presently
The massive volume of the world
Closes again.

Upon that book I swear
To abide by what it teaches:
Gospels of ugliness and waste,
Of towering voids, of soiled gusts,
Of a shrieking to be faced
Full into, eyes astream with cold—

With cold?
All right then. With self-knowledge.

Indoors at last, the pages of *Time* are apt
To open, and the illustrated mayor of New York,
Given a glimpse of how and where I work,
To note yet one more house that can be scrapped.

Unwillingly I picture
My walls weathering in the general view.
It is not even as though the new
Buildings did very much for architecture.

Suppose they did. The sickness of our time requires
That these as well be blasted in their prime.
You would think the simple fact of having lasted
Threatened our cities like mysterious fires.

There are certain phrases which to use in a poem
Is like rubbing silver with quicksilver. Bright

15 But facile, the glamour deadens overnight.
For instance, how 'the sickness of our time'

Enhances, then debases, what I feel.
At my desk I swallow in a glass of water
No longer cordial, scarcely wet, a pill
They had told me not to take until much later.

With the result that back into my imagination
The city glides, like cities seen from the air,
Mere smoke and sparkle to the passenger
Having in mind another destination

Which now is not that honey-slow descent
Of the Champs-Elysées, her hand in his,
But the dull need to make some kind of house
Out of the life lived, out of the love spent.

JAMES MERRILL

Depression

My mattress floats in an ocean of newspapers
through the eternal night of the fifty states.
On the ocean floor generals and editors
ride sharks through forests of diseased sea anemones,
sabreing Sioux and negroes and Vietnamese.

I try desperately to sleep, to dream, to vomit—
anything to shut out the hissing sound
of limbs and heads as they bob to the surface
from the fathomless layers of print.
I expect any moment the heads of my children.

WILLIAM WITHERUP

216 Them, Crying

In the well-fed cage-sound of diesels,
Here, in the cab's boxed wind,
He is called to by something beyond
His life. In the sun's long haul
Of light, each week at this place,
He sings to the truck's eight wheels

But at night it is worse than useless:
The great building shoots and holds

Its rays, and he hears, through the engine,
Through the killed words of his own song,
Them: them crying. Unmarried, unchildlike,
Half-bearded and foul-mouthed, he feels
His hands lean away to the right
And bear the truck spiraling down

To the four streets going around
And around and around the hospital.

He sits, and the voices are louder,
An awakening, part-song sound
Calling anyone out of the life
He thought he led: a sound less than twelve
Years ago, which wakes to the less-than-nothing
Of a bent glass straw in a glass

With small sleepless bubbles stuck to it:
Which feels a new mouth sewn shut

In a small body's back or its side
And would free some angelic voice
From the black crimped thread,

17

The snipped cat-whiskers of a wound—
A sound that can find no way
To attack the huge, orderly flowers.

At one-thirty he is drawn in,
Drawn in, drawn in and in,

Listening, through dozens of Bakelite floors
And walls, brogan-stepping along
Through green-tiled nightlighted rooms
Where implements bake in glass cases,
Through halls full of cloudy test tubes,
Up and down self-service elevators

That open both sides at once,
Through closets of lubricants,

Through a black beehive of typed labels,
Through intimate theatres
Scrubbed down with Lysol and salt,
Through a sordid district of pails,
Until, on the third floor rear
Of the donated Southeast Wing,

He comes on a man holding wrongly
A doll with feigning-closed eyes,

And a fat woman, hat in her lap,
Has crashed through a chairback to sleep.
Unbelonging, he circles their circle;
Then, as though a stitch broke
In his stomach, he wheels and goes through
The double-frosted warning-marked door.

Twelve parents at bay intone
In the brain waves that wash around heroes:

218

Come, stripped to your T-shirt sleeves,
Your coveralls, blue jeans, or chains,
Your helmets or thickening haircuts,
Your white coats, your rock-pounding foreheads,
For our children lie there beyond us
In the still, foreign city of pain

Singing backward into the world
To those never seen before,

Old cool-handed doctors and young ones,
Capped girls bearing vessels of glucose,
Ginger ward boys, pan handlers, technicians,
Thieves, nightwalkers, truckers, and drunkards
Who must hear, not listening, them:
Them, crying: for they rise only unto

Those few who transcend themselves,
The superhuman tenderness of strangers.

JAMES DICKEY

The Human Condition

In this motel where I was told to wait,
The television screen is stood before
The picture window. Nothing could be more
Use to a man than knowing where he's at,
And I know, but pace the day in doubt
Between my looking in and looking out.

Though snow, along the snowy road, cars pass
Going both ways, and pass behind the screen
Where heads of heroes sometimes can be seen
And sometimes cars, that speed across the glass.

19   Once I saw world and thought exactly meet,
But only in a picture by Magritte,

A picture of a picture, by Magritte,
Wherein a landscape on an easel stands
Before a window opening on a land-
scape, and the pair of them a perfect fit,
Silent and mad. You know right off, the room
Before that scene was always an empty room.

And that is now the room in which I stand
Waiting, or walk, and sometimes try to sleep.
The day falls into darkness while I keep
The TV going; headlights blaze behind
Its legendary traffic, love and hate,
In this motel where I was told to wait.

HOWARD NEMEROV

The Journey of a Poem
Compared to all the Sad
Variety of Travel

A poem moves forward,
    Like the passages and percussions of trains in progress
    A pattern of recurrence, a hammer of repetitive occurrence

        a slow less and less heard
        Low thunder under all passengers
Steel sounds tripping and tripled and
Grinding, revolving, gripping, turning, and returning
As the flung carpet of the wide countryside spreads out on
        each side in billows

220   And in isolation, rolled out, white house, red barn, squat silo,
Pasture, hill, meadow and woodland pasture
And the stripped poles step fast past the train windows
Second after second takes snapshots, clicking,
Into the dangled boxes of glinting windows
Snapshots and selections, rejections, at angles of shadows
A small town: a shop's sign—GARAGE; and then white gates
Where waiting cars wait with the unrest of trembling
Breathing hard and idling, until the slow descent
Of the red cones of sunset: a dead march: a slow tread and
    heavy

Of the slowed horses of Apollo
—Until the slowed horses of Apollo go over the horizon
And all things are parked, slowly or willingly
into the customary or at random places

DELMORE SCHWARTZ

Carmen Saeculare

Shuffle and reshuffle. Still the times will stack
The *dies irae* ready in the deck.

Grown various-minded as a hand-grenade,
I feel like bursting, or a Grant-in-Aid;
See Europe first, and let Fort Knox go hang;
I enterprise for freedom from harangue.

The tube's electrons dance, the ball descends
Upon the moment when December ends;
The lemmings of the Square dissolve in snow,
The set clicks off, around the room we go.

One Pliny died, the other Pliny wrote
His friend a proper scientific note;

Before the mountain bursts, I want to see
How I will look when ashes cover me.

Dog or human huddled in its crape,
The stuff is faithful to the smothered shape;
Pompeii's museum, with its bread gone black,
Substantiates the mind it summons back.

Ordo vagorum, visaed by the wind,
Welcome a scholar grown undisciplined;
The military virtues of your rule
Will put me to the roadways for a school.

Some say Odysseus, wild with settled age,
Set sail with Helen fleeing from her cage;
Scornful of all his patient pain had won,
He turned his prow to Egypt and the sun.

JOHN TAYLOR

The Honored Dead

I saw it rise, a stunted, soot-encrusted
shaft, embedded in a mounded isle
washed by the surf of cobblestones within
an intersection fed by streets and rained on
by the dust of factories. The list
of names was long; the dedication, firm.
"Their sacrifice," it said, "would be forever
green in memories of men." The gold
stars near the names had broken off, but dust
and soot had filled the open holes. Someone
had thought of an eternal fire, but someone
else had disagreed: a hole remained,
stuffed with débris. The lonely atoll had
no turf, only bare earth that glittered with

222
the silica of grit and sparkled with
the vivid hues of bottle caps and crumpled
candy wraps. The rows of houses on
opposing banks were empty; their windows—
those not boarded—stared blindly as the strangers
passed, ignored the roar of cars, the blare
of horns, the scream of factory whistles and
the tread of trucks. The neighborhood was zoned
"industrial" after the Second War.
The residents had moved to other homes
with plots of lawn and trees and asphalt streets
and cleaner air than that these names had known.
By now their loss has ceased to be the wound
it was when notice of the government's
regret was fresh and gold stars were in place.

But now it's clear the island is a waste
of space. The neighborhood's an eyesore, too.
On that there's clear agreement among all.
But no one lives there now. The old, who had
the time to beautify the homes, are gone;
the rest drive in and out. A program must be
drawn up for the block. The houses are
mere shells, a breeding ground for vice. Someone
proposed to raze the site and build an asphalt
parking lot, which might resolve the city's
double fears of crime and urban blight.

THOMAS DOULIS

Supplementary Poems:
For comparison and discussion

Chicago
Carl Sandburg

GLOSSARY

accent   designation of emphasized or stressed syllables and/or phrases in a line of verse

allegory   a narrative, either in verse or prose, wherein the principals (events, objects, or characters) identify abstract qualities which comprise a body of belief. Allegorical characters are a particular kind of *personification*; e.g., a character named Vice who epitomizes that particular abstract quality.

alliteration   repetition of initial consonants, as in "The *full* streams *feed* on *flower* rushes." (See p. 58.)

allusion   reference to literary, historical, mythological, biblical, or other commonly shared cultural experience; used by the poet as an economical means of evoking or reinforcing desired responses traditionally associated with the subject referred to. (See p. 27 ff.)

anapest   a metrical *foot* consisting of two unaccented syllables followed by one accented syllable (xx/). (See pp. 53, 56.)

assonance   marked repetition of similar vowel sounds, usually appearing in the middle or at the ends of words, as in "So all day long the noise of the battle rolled"

ballad   a *narrative* poem generally categorized as either folk or literary. The **folk ballad** is a poem, usually anonymous in origin, designed to be sung and transmitted orally, concerned with a single climactic incident, often violent and/or tragic, episodically dramatized in a series of two- or four-line stanzas, sometimes repeated or interspersed with a recurring *refrain*. The narrative is spare, economical, with no attempt at analysis, interpretation, or editorializing. (For an example of a modern ballad, see "Birmingham Sunday," p. 149.) The **literary ballad** is a more sophisticated version of the folk ballad, retaining a close adherence to the traditional stanzaic structure and narrative character but not intended to be sung; e.g., "The Rime of the Ancient Mariner."

blank verse   unrhymed verse written in iambic pentameter measure

cadence   nonmetrical rhythm established by accenting word groups or phrases rather than syllables; characteristic of *free verse*. (See pp. 57–58.)

caesura   a pause in a line of poetry, usually appearing in the middle of the line, which may or may not be indicated by punctuation; schematized by //: "So long lives this//and this give life to thee"

consonance   marked repetition of consonant sounds, appearing for the most part in the middle or at the ends of words, as in "As virtuous men pass mildly away,/And whisper to their souls to go"

couplet   a pair of rhymed lines

dactyl   a metrical *foot* consisting of one accented syllable followed by two unaccented syllables (/xx). (See p. 53.)

decasyllabic   a line of verse having ten syllables

dimeter   a two-*foot* line

dirge   see *elegy*

dramatic monologue   a poem wherein a single character, who is not the poet himself, addresses a listener in the poem who never speaks himself—thus the reference to "monologue." The drama is created by the fact that the monologue is delivered at a critical moment in a situation and is so conceived as to focus the reader's attention on aspects of the personality or temperament of the speaker, aspects which the speaker, ironically, fails to recognize in himself. Examples may be found in much of Robert Browning's poetry ("The Bishop Orders His Tomb at St. Praxed's Church," to name one) and T. S. Eliot's "The Love Song of J. Alfred Prufrock."

elegy   a formal, meditative poem lamenting the loss of someone through death. Differs from a *dirge* in that the dirge is a rela-

227

tively short expression of such grief while the elegy is a sustained expression of the same emotion. (See "war, war" and "Shot With a Hot Rot Gun.") A particular type of elegy is the **pastoral elegy,** a form governed by a series of conventions which include a pastoral setting, invocation of the muses, nature joining in mourning, the passage of the "shepherd," questions about corrupt conditions in the poet's time, and a shift in tone at the end from grief to joy at the poet's realization that the subject has gained a better life through death; e.g. John Milton's "Lycidas."

end-stopped lines lines which end with a natural pause, dictated by either the grammatical or sense completion, or both, of those lines

> How sleep the brave who sink to rest
> By all their country's wishes blest!

enjambment a run-on line, one with no punctuation or other significant pause at the end

epic a long *narrative poem* dealing with a subject of great significance to a nation or race and characterized by numerous conventions: characters and actions of heroic proportions, an elevated style, and material drawn from the legends that are at the foundations of every culture; e.g., *Beowulf, Iliad, Odyssey, Paradise Lost.* The **mock epic** is an ironic treatment of the epic conventions. It uses formalities of the epic style to present, usually for comic purposes, trivial materials; e.g., Alexander Pope's "The Rape of the Lock."

feminine rhyme rhyme in which the rhyming stressed syllables are followed by identical unstressed syllables. If only one identical unstressed syllable follows, we have an instance of double rhyme (weary – dreary, trumpet – crumpet). If two unstressed syllables identical to the unstressed syllables in the corresponding rhyming word follow the accented syllable, we have triple rhyme (lucidity – validity, erroneous – felonious).

foot basic unit of measure in *scansion*. Composed of a combination of either one or two unstressed syllables and a single stressed syllable, except in the case of the *spondee* or *pyrrhic* feet. (See *anapest, dactyl, iamb, trochee.*) (See also p. 55ff.)

free verse poetry free of dependence upon traditional English metrics for its rhythm. Whatever rhythm it does contain evolves primarily from the combination of words and phrases the poet employs rather than from syllabic accenting. (See *cadence.*)

hexameter   a six-*foot* line

heptameter   a seven-*foot* line

hyperbole   obvious overstatement or exaggeration of fact for the sake of emphasis. (See pp. 31–33.)

iamb   a metrical *foot* consisting of one unaccented syllable followed by a single accented syllable (x/). (See pp. 52–53.)

imagery   language that attempts to vividly present a sense impression. This term is also used to describe connotative diction, the compressive characteristic of figurative language. (See pp. 5–8.)

irony   contrast between what is and what is intended. Three specific kinds of irony are (1) **dramatic irony,** where there is a contradiction between what is said by characters and what the author means; (2) **situational irony,** where there is a contradiction between expectation and fulfillment in a situation; (3) **verbal irony,** where there is a contradiction between what the speaker says and what he actually means. (See pp. 38–41.)

limerick   a form of light playful poetry, five *anapestic* lines long, with the first, second, and fifth lines rhymed *trimeter* and the third and fourth lines rhymed *dimeter*:

> There was an old man with a beard,
> Who said, "It is just as I feared,
> Two owls and a hen,
> Four larks and a wren,
> Have all built their nests in my beard!"

lyric   originally a verse to be sung to the accompaniment of a lyre; now used to describe any short poem which is designed to capture a personal state of feeling or thought rather than to narrate a tale. Extremely subjective, the lyric has been described as a "sung moment," the projection of a "single, unified impression." Lyric characteristics are common to most poetic forms, such as the *sonnet, ode, elegy,* and *dramatic monologue;* consequently, these forms are also described as lyric poetry. However, they are distinct species of lyric verse by virtue of particular conventions governing their structure and purpose.

GLOSSARY

229 **masculine rhyme**   rhyme in which the stressed syllable governing the rhymed sound is not followed by any other syllable (still – hill, suffice – precise).

metaphor   a figure of speech that equates two (or more) usually dissimilar things; e.g., "The sun is a balloon." (See pp. 9–11.)

meter   the rhythm of a line in terms of the prevalent kind of *foot* and the number of feet in the line. (See pp. 52–57.)

metonymy   the use of something closely associated with an idea or experience, but not necessarily an integral part of that idea, to represent the entire idea; e.g., "The pen is mightier than the sword." (See *synecdoche*.)

narrative poetry   poetry which tells a story. (See *ballad* and *epic*.)

octave   an eight-line stanza

ode   an extended *lyric* poem characterized by an intellectual and dignified loftiness of *tone*. Among the conventions governing this form is the stanzaic and metrical division of the poem into various combinations of strophe, antistrophe, and epode. There are three basic types of ode in English verse—**Pindaric, Horation,** and **irregular.**

onomatopoeia   the use of words that imitate or sound like the meaning, as *crash, thud, buzz*. (See p. 59.)

oxymoron   a combination of terms which in normal usage is contradictory, as in "painful pleasure" and "quiet violence"

paradox   a statement or situation that seems to be, but is not necessarily, contradictory; e.g., ". . . when war is peace" (from "19??," pp. 132–133.)

pentameter   a five-*foot* line

personification   ascribing human characteristics to an idea or nonhuman, as well as to inanimate objects. (See pp. 12–13.)

pyrrhic   a metrical *foot* of two unstressed syllables (xx)

quatrain   a four-line stanza. Among the more familiar rhyme schemes for this length stanza are *abcb, abab, aabb*.

refrain   a phrase or a line of poetry repeated at intervals, frequently appearing at the end of each stanza. A common characteristic of the sung ballad, both traditional and modern. (See "Dangling Conversation," p. 87.)

230   **rhythm**   the "flow" of a line of poetry, the movement within it, much like "beat" in music. It is usually derived from the metrical structure of the line; i.e., the type and number of feet that compose the line. However, it may also be established through syntactical variations such as pauses and run-ons. (See *meter, cadence, caesura, enjambment.*) (See pp. 52–59.)

   rhyme   generally speaking, the similarity of sounds in two or more lines, wherein each of the stressed syllables producing the rhyming sound occupy approximately the same position in their respective lines. When discussing rhyme, one may describe it in any of the following terms, either singularly or, where applicable, in combination:

     perfect rhyme—rhyme based on stressed syllables wherein the vowels and succeeding consonants composing them are identical. The consonants preceding, however, must be different. (cat – rat, bore – more, ring – sing, running – punning)

     slant rhyme—corresponding sounds that are similar but not precisely the same. Also known as *approximate rhyme*, it is achieved by corresponding only the final consonant sounds and having different initial vowels and consonants (soul – ball, groaned – crooned – ground).

     beginning rhyme—corresponding sounds occurring in the first syllable or syllables of lines

     internal rhyme—corresponding sounds which occur somewhere other than at the beginnings or ends of lines

     end rhyme—corresponding sounds occurring at the ends of lines

     masculine rhyme (See p. 229.)

     feminine rhyme (See p. 227.)

   scansion   the process of determining the *meter* of a line of poetry (See p. 55.)

   sestet   a six-line stanza

   simile   a figure of speech which states, through use of such terms as *like, as, so,* a comparison between different quantities or qualities. (See p. 9.)

   sonnet   a fixed form of poetry composed of fourteen lines of iambic pentameter. Though various poets, Keats and Milton among them, have modified the sonnet form for their particular purposes at one time or another, the two standard schemes that prevail are the English (Shakespearean) and the Italian (Petrarchan). The **English sonnet** consists of three *quatrains* and a *couplet*, rhymed *ababcdcdefefgg*. The first quatrain usually establishes the argument or theme; the second and third quatrains develop or present variations on that theme; and the couplet sums up or resolves it. In the **Petrarchan sonnet**, the scheme is considered in two parts: an *octave* (the first eight lines rhymed *abbaabba*) and a *sestet* (the last six lines rhymed in various ways, two of which are *cdcdcd* and *cdecde*). In this latter form, the theme is established in the octave and the conclusions the poet reaches about that theme are presented in the sestet.

spondee   two adjacent accented syllables (//)

symbol   a concrete object or action used to represent an abstract concept. Many symbols are conventional; that is, the society or culture has traditionally attributed particular significance to specific symbols; e.g., the flag as symbol of a nation. But frequently in literature, the artist creates his own symbols, shaping the details of his work so that they are given a symbolic force not commonly attributed to them, as in "Santa Claus," p. 61. (See also pp. 12–21.)

synecdoche   an integral part of something used to represent the entire thing; e.g., fifty voices – fifty people. (See *metonymy*.) (See p. 23.)

tetrameter   a four-*foot* line

tone   the emotional attitude of the poem. Recognition of it is extremely important for defining and interpreting the author's meaning or intent. If one is quickly able to determine whether the tone of a poem is ironic, joyful, somber, fearful, angry, etc., he has significantly reduced the number of possible interpretations available to him. (See p. 38 ff.)

trimeter   a three-line foot

triplet or tercet   a three-line stanza

trochee   a metrical *foot* consisting of one accented syllable followed by a single unaccented syllable (/x). (See p. 53, 56–57.)

232 **understatement** saying less than one means; making a weaker statement about a subject than that subject warrants, as in the last line of "A Song About Major Eatherly," pp. 79, 85, and "Outside A Small Circle of Friends," p. 111. (See *hyperbole*.) (See also pp. 89–91.)

INDEX OF POETS

INDEX OF POEMS

INDEX OF FIRST LINES